Advances in AI
And Autonomous Vehicles:
Cybernetic Self-Driving Cars

Practical Advances in Artificial Intelligence (AI) and Machine Learning

Dr. Lance B. Eliot, MBA, PhD

Disclaimer: This book is presented solely for educational and entertainment purposes. The author and publisher are not offering it as legal, accounting, or other professional services advice. The author and publisher make no representations or warranties of any kind and assume no liabilities of any kind with respect to the accuracy or completeness of the contents and specifically disclaim any implied warranties of merchantability or fitness of use for a particular purpose. Neither the author nor the publisher shall be held liable or responsible to any person or entity with respect to any loss or incidental or consequential damages caused, or alleged to have been caused, directly or indirectly, by the information or programs contained herein. Every company is different and the advice and strategies contained herein may not be suitable for your situation.

DEDICATION

To my wonderful daughter, Lauren, and my wonderful son, Michael.

Forest fortuna adiuvat (from the Latin; good fortune favors the brave).

CONTENTS

Lance B. Eliot

ACKNOWLEDGMENTS

I have been the beneficiary of advice and counsel by many friends, colleagues, family, investors, and many others. I want to thank everyone that has aided me throughout my career. I write from the heart and the head, having experienced first-hand what it means to have others around you that support you during the good times and the tough times.

To Warren Bennis, one of my doctoral advisors and ultimately a colleague, I offer my deepest thanks and appreciation, especially for his calm and insightful wisdom and support.

To Mark Stevens and his generous efforts toward funding and supporting the USC Stevens Center for Innovation.

To Lloyd Greif and the USC Lloyd Greif Center for Entrepreneurial Studies for their ongoing encouragement of founders and entrepreneurs.

To Peter Drucker, William Wang, Aaron Levie, Peter Kim, Jon Kraft, Cindy Crawford, Jenny Ming, Steve Milligan, Chis Underwood, Frank Gehry, and Colonel Sanders, Buzz Aldrin, Steve Forbes, Bill Thompson, Dave Dillon, Alan Fuerstman, Larry Ellison, Jim Sinegal, John Sperling, Mark Stevenson, Anand Nallathambi, Thomas Barrack, Jr., and many other innovators and leaders that I have met and gained mightily from doing so.

Thanks to Ed Trainor, Kevin Anderson, James Hickey, Wendell Jones, Ken Harris, DuWayne Peterson, Mike Brown, Jim Thornton, Abhi Beniwal, Al Biland, John Nomura, Eliot Weinman, John Desmond, and many others for their unwavering support during my career.

And most of all thanks as always to Lauren and Michael, for their ongoing support and for having seen me writing and heard much of this material during the many months involved in writing it. To their patience and willingness to listen.

Lance B. Eliot

INTRODUCTION

This is a book about recent advances in Artificial Intelligence (AI) and Machine Learning (ML) that are enabling the advent of truly autonomous vehicles, which means vehicles that can control themselves and that do not require and nor rely upon human intervention to perform their driving tasks (or, that <u>allow</u> for human intervention, but only *require* human intervention in very limited ways).

I am particularly focused on those advances that pertain to self-driving cars. The phrase "autonomous vehicles" is often used to refer to any kind of vehicle, whether it is ground-based or in the air or sea, and whether it is a cargo hauling trailer truck or a conventional passenger car. Though the aspects described in this book are certainly applicable to all kinds of autonomous vehicles, I am focused more so here on cars.

Indeed, I am especially known for my role in aiding the advancement of self-driving cars. In addition to writing software, designing and developing systems and software for self-driving cars, I also speak and write quite a bit about the topic. This book is a collection of some of my more technologically advanced essays. For those of you that might have seen my essays posted elsewhere, I have updated them and integrated them into this book as one handy cohesive package.

There is a companion book that I wrote that covers other fundamentals about self-driving cars, and which is not quite as advanced as the material herein. That book is provocatively entitled **Self-Driving Cars: "The Mother of All AI Projects"** and which gained its title by the aspect that the CEO of Apple proclaimed that developing a self-driving car is "the mother of all AI projects," and is something I've been saying for many years.

For the introduction here to this book, I am going to borrow my introduction from that companion book, since it does a good job of laying out the landscape of self-driving cars and my overall viewpoints on the topic. The remainder of the book is all new material that does not appear in the companion book.

INTRODUCTION TO SELF-DRIVING CARS

This is a book about self-driving cars. Someday in the future, we'll all have self-driving cars and this book will perhaps seem antiquated, but right now, we are at the forefront of the self-driving car wave. Daily news bombards us with flashes of new announcements by one car maker or another and leaves the impression that within the next few weeks or maybe months that the self-driving car will be here. A casual non-technical reader would assume from these news flashes that in fact we must be on the cusp of a true self-driving car.

Here's a real news flash: We are still quite a distance from having a true self-driving car. It is years to go before we get there.

Why is that? Because a true self-driving car is akin to a moonshot. In the same manner that getting us to the moon was an incredible feat, likewise can it be said for achieving a true self-driving car. Anybody that suggests or even brashly states that the true self-driving car is nearly here should be viewed with great skepticism. Indeed, you'll see that I often tend to use the word "hogwash" or "crock" when I assess much of the decidedly *fake news* about self-driving cars. Those of us on the inside know that what is often reported to the outside is malarkey. Few of the insiders are willing to say so. I have no such hesitation.

Indeed, I've been writing a popular blog post about self-driving cars and hitting hard on those that try to wave their hands and pretend that we are on the imminent verge of true self-driving cars. For many years, I've been known as the AI Insider. Besides writing about AI, I also develop AI software. I do what I describe. It also gives me insights into what others that are doing AI are really doing versus what it is said they are doing.

Many faithful readers had asked me to pull together my insightful short essays and put them into a book, which you are now holding in your hands. I was trying to decide what title to give to the book, and fortunately something happened that prompted me to use the title you now see. Making a true self-driving car is "the mother of all AI projects" seems like an apt way to describe this moonshot journey, and I explain in a moment what especially sparked me to use that title for this book.

For those of you that have been reading my essays over the years, this collection not only puts them together into one handy package, I also updated the essays and added new material. For those of you that are new to the topic of self-driving cars and AI, I hope you find these essays approachable and informative. I also tend to have a writing style with a bit of a voice, and so you'll see that I am times have a wry sense of humor and also like to poke at conformity.

As a former professor and founder of an AI research lab, I for many years wrote in the formal language of academic writing. I published in referred journals and served as an editor for several AI journals. This writing here is not of the nature, and I have adopted a different and more informal style for these essays. That being said, I also do mention from time-to-time more rigorous material on AI and encourage you all to dig into those deeper and more formal materials if so interested.

I am also an AI practitioner. This means that I write AI software for a living. Currently, I head-up the Cybernetics Self-Driving Car Institute, where we are developing AI software for self-driving cars. I am excited to also report that my son, also a software engineer, heads-up our Cybernetics Self-Driving Car Lab. What I have helped to start, and for which he is an integral part, ultimately he will carry long into the future after I have retired. My daughter, a marketing whiz, also is integral to our efforts as head of our Marketing group. She too will carry forward the legacy now being formulated.

For those of you that are reading this book and have a penchant for writing code, you might consider taking a look at the open source code available for self-driving cars. This is a handy place to start learning how to develop AI for self-driving cars. There are also many new educational courses spring forth.

There is a growing body of those wanting to learn about and develop self-driving cars, and a growing body of colleges, labs, and other avenues by which you can learn about self-driving cars.

This book will provide a foundation of aspects that I think will get you ready for those kinds of more advanced training opportunities. If you've already taken those classes, you'll likely find these essays especially interesting as they offer a perspective that I am betting few other instructors or faculty offered to you. These are challenging essays that ask you to think beyond the conventional about self-driving cars.

THE MOTHER OF ALL AI PROJECTS

In June 2017, Apple CEO Tim Cook came out and finally admitted that Apple has been working on a self-driving car. As you'll see in my essays, Apple was enmeshed in secrecy about their self-driving car efforts. We have only been able to read the tea leaves and guess at what Apple has been up to. The notion of an iCar has been floating for quite a while, and self-driving engineers and researchers have been signing tight-lipped Non-Disclosure Agreements (NDA's) to work on projects at Apple that were as shrouded in mystery as any military invasion plans might be.

Tim Cook said something that many others in the Artificial Intelligence

(AI) field have been saying, namely, the creation of a self-driving car has got to be the mother of all AI projects. In other words, it is in fact a tremendous moonshot for AI. If a self-driving car can be crafted and the AI works as we hope, it means that we have made incredible strides with AI and that therefore it opens many other worlds of potential breakthrough accomplishments that AI can solve.

Is this hyperbole? Am I just trying to make AI seem like a miracle worker and so provide self-aggrandizing statements for those of us writing the AI software for self-driving cars? No, it is not hyperbole. Developing a true self-driving car is really, really, really hard to do. Let me take a moment to explain why. As a side note, I realize that the Apple CEO is known for at times uttering hyperbole, and he had previously said for example that the year 2012 was "the mother of all years," and he had said that the release of iOS 10 was "the mother of all releases" – all of which does suggest he likes to use the handy "mother of" expression. But, I assure you, in terms of true self-driving cars, he has hit the nail on the head. For sure.

When you think about a moonshot and how we got to the moon, there are some identifiable characteristics and those same aspects can be applied to creating a true self-driving car. You'll notice that I keep putting the word "true" in front of the self-driving car expression. I do so because as per my essay about the various levels of self-driving cars (see Chapter 3), there are some self-driving cars that are only somewhat of a self-driving car. The somewhat versions are ones that require a human driver to be ready to intervene. In my view, that's not a true self-driving car. A true self-driving car is one that requires no human driver intervention at all. It is a car that can entirely undertake via automation the driving task without any human driver needed. This is the essence of what is known as a Level 5 self-driving car. We are currently at the Level 2 and Level 3 mark, and not yet at Level 5.

Getting to the moon involved aspects such as having big stretch goals, incremental progress, experimentation, innovation, and so on. Let's review how this applied to the moonshot of the bygone era, and how it applies to the self-driving car moonshot of today.

Big Stretch Goal

Trying to take a human and deliver the human to the moon, and bring them back, safely, was an extremely large stretch goal at the time. No one knew whether it could be done. The technology wasn't available yet. The cost was huge. The determination would need to be fierce. Etc. To reach a Level 5 self-driving car is going to be the same. It is a big stretch goal. We can readily get to the Level 3, and we are able to see the Level 4 just up ahead, but a Level 5 is still an unknown as to if it is doable. It should eventually be doable and in the same way that we thought we'd eventually get to the moon, but when it will occur is a different story.

Incremental Progress

Getting to the moon did not happen overnight in one fell swoop. It took years and years of incremental progress to get there. Likewise for self-driving cars. Google has famously been striving to get to the Level 5, and pretty much been willing to forgo dealing with the intervening levels, but most of the other self-driving car makers are doing the incremental route. Let's get a good Level 2 and a somewhat Level 3 going. Then, let's improve the Level 3 and get a somewhat Level 4 going. Then, let's improve the Level 4 and finally arrive at a Level 5. This seems to be the prevalent way that we are going to achieve the true self-driving car.

Experimentation

You likely know that there were various experiments involved in perfecting the approach and technology to get to the moon. As per making incremental progress, we first tried to see if we could get a rocket to go into space and safety return, then put a monkey in there, then with a human, then we went all the way to the moon but didn't land, and finally we arrived at the mission that actually landed on the moon. Self-driving cars are the same way. We are doing simulations of self-driving cars. We do testing of self-driving cars on private land under controlled situations. We do testing of self-driving cars on public roadways, often having to meet regulatory requirements including for example having an engineer or equivalent in the car to take over the controls if needed. And so on. Experiments big and small are needed to figure out what works and what doesn't.

Innovation

There are already some advances in AI that are allowing us to progress toward self-driving cars (see Chapter 1). We are going to need even more advances. Innovation in all aspects of technology are going to be required to achieve a true self-driving car. By no means do we already have everything in-hand that we need to get there. Expect new inventions and new approaches, new algorithms, etc.

Setbacks

Most of the pundits are avoiding talking about potential setbacks in the progress toward self-driving cars. Getting to the moon involved many setbacks, some of which you never have heard of and were buried at the time so as to not dampen enthusiasm and funding for getting to the moon. A recurring theme in many of my included essays is that there are going to be setbacks as we try to arrive at a true self-driving car. Take a deep breath and be ready. I just hope the setbacks don't completely stop progress. I am sure that it will cause progress to alter in a manner that we've not yet seen in the self-driving car field. I liken the self-driving car of today to the excitement everyone had for Uber when it first got going. Today, we have a different view of Uber and with each passing day there are more regulations to the ride sharing business and more concerns raised. The darling child only stays a darling until finally that child acts up. It will happen the same with self-driving cars.

SELF-DRIVING CARS CHALLENGES

But what exactly makes things so hard to have a true self-driving car, you might be asking. You have seen cruise control for years and years. You've lately seen cars that can do parallel parking. You've seen YouTube videos of Tesla drivers that put their hands out the window as their car zooms along the highway, and seen to therefore be in a self-driving car. Aren't we just needing to put a few more sensors onto a car and then we'll have in-hand a true self-driving car? Nope.

Consider for a moment the nature of the driving task. We don't just let anyone at any age drive a car. Worldwide, most countries won't license a driver until the age of 18, though many do allow a learner's permit at the age of 15 or 16. Some suggest that a younger age would be physically too small to reach the controls of the car. Though this might be the case, we could easily adjust the controls to allow for younger aged and thus smaller stature. It's not their physical size that matters. It's their cognitive development that matters.

To drive a car, you need to be able to reason about the car, what the car can and cannot do. You need to know how to operate the car. You need to know about how other cars on the road drive. You need to know what is allowed in driving such as speed limits and driving within marked lanes. You need to be able to react to situations and be able to avoid getting into accidents. You need to ascertain when to hit your brakes, when to steer clear of a pedestrian, and how to keep from ramming that motorcyclist that just cut you off.

Many of us had taken courses on driving. We studied about driving and took driver training. We had to take a test and pass it to be able to drive. The point being that though most adults take the driving task for granted, and we often "mindlessly" drive our cars, there is a significant amount of cognitive effort that goes into driving a car. After a while, it becomes second nature. You don't especially think about how you drive, you just do it. But, if you watch a novice driver, say a teenager learning to drive, you suddenly realize that there is a lot more complexity to it than we seem to realize.

Furthermore, driving is a very serious task. I recall when my daughter and son first learned to drive. They are both very conscientious people. They wanted to make sure that whatever they did, they did well, and that they did not harm anyone. Every day, when you get into a car, it is probably around 4,000 pounds of hefty metal and plastics (about two tons), and it is a lethal weapon. Think about it. You drive down the street in an object that weighs two tons and with the engine it can accelerate and ram into anything you want to hit. The damage a car can inflict is very scary. Both my children were surprised that they were being given the right to maneuver this monster of a beast that could cause tremendous harm entirely by merely letting go of the steering wheel for a moment or taking your eyes off the road.

In fact, in the United States alone there are about 30,000 deaths per year by auto accidents, which is around 100 per day. Given that there are about 263 million cars in the United States, I am actually more amazed that the number of fatalities is not a lot higher. During my morning commute, I look at all the thousands of cars on the freeway around me, and I think that if all of them decided to go zombie and drive in a crazy maniac way, there would be many people dead. Somehow, incredibly, each day, most people drive relatively safely. To me, that's a miracle right there. Getting millions and millions of people to be safe and sane when behind the wheel of a two ton mobile object, it's a feat that we as a society should admire with pride.

So, hopefully you are in agreement that the driving task requires a great deal of cognition. You don't' need to be especially smart to drive a car, and we've done quite a bit to make car driving viable for even the average dolt. There isn't an IQ test that you need to take to drive a car. If you can read and write, and pass a test, you pretty much can legally drive a car. There are of course some that drive a car and are not legally permitted to do so, plus there are private areas such as farms where drivers are young, but for public roadways in the United States, you can be generally of average intelligence (or less) and be able to legally drive.

This though makes it seem like the cognitive effort must not be much. If the cognitive effort was truly hard, wouldn't we only have Einstein's that could drive a car? We have made sure to keep the driving task as simple as we can, by making the controls easy and relatively standardized, and by having roads that are relatively standardized, and so on. It is as though Disneyland has put their Autopia into the real-world, by us all as a society agreeing that roads will be a certain way, and we'll all abide by the various rules of driving.

A modest cognitive task by a human is still something that stymies AI.

You certainly know that AI has been able to beat chess players and be good at other kinds of games. This type of narrow cognition is not what car driving is about. Car driving is much wider. It requires knowledge about the world, which a chess playing AI system does not need to know. The cognitive aspects of driving are on the one hand seemingly simple, but at the same time require layer upon layer of knowledge about cars, people, roads, rules, and a myriad of other "common sense" aspects. We don't have any AI systems today that have that same kind of breadth and depth of awareness and knowledge.

As revealed in my essays, the self-driving car of today is using trickery to do particular tasks. It is all very narrow in operation. Plus, it currently assumes that a human driver is ready to intervene. It is like a child that we have taught to stack blocks, but we are needed to be right there in case the child stacks them too high and they begin to fall over. AI of today is brittle, it is narrow, and it does not approach the cognitive abilities of humans. This is why the true self-driving car is somewhere out in the future.

Another aspect to the driving task is that it is not solely a mind exercise. You do need to use your senses to drive. You use your eyes a vision sensors to see the road ahead. You vision capability is like a streaming video, which your brain needs to continually analyze as you drive. Where is the road? Is there a pedestrian in the way? Is there another car ahead of you? Your senses are relying a flood of info to your brain. Self-driving cars are trying to do the same, by using cameras, radar, ultrasound, and lasers. This is an attempt at mimicking how humans have senses and sensory apparatus.

Thus, the driving task is mental and physical. You use your senses, you use your arms and legs to manipulate the controls of the car, and you use your brain to assess the sensory info and direct your limbs to act upon the controls of the car. This all happens instantly. If you've ever perhaps gotten something in your eye and only had one eye available to drive with, you suddenly realize how dependent upon vision you are. If you have a broken foot with a cast, you suddenly realize how hard it is to control the brake pedal and the accelerator. If you've taken medication and your brain is maybe sluggish, you suddenly realize how much mental strain is required to drive a car.

An AI system that plays chess only needs to be focused on playing chess. The physical aspects aren't important because usually a human moves the chess pieces or the chessboard is shown on an electronic display. Using AI for a more life-and-death task such as analyzing MRI images of patients, this again does not require physical capabilities and instead is done by examining images of bits.

Driving a car is a true life-and-death task. It is a use of AI that can easily and at any moment produce death. For those colleagues of mine that are developing this AI, as am I, we need to keep in mind the somber aspects of this. We are producing software that will have in its virtual hands the lives of the occupants of the car, and the lives of those in other nearby cars, and the lives of nearby pedestrians, etc. Chess is not usually a life-or-death matter.

Driving is all around us. Cars are everywhere. Most of today's AI applications involve only a small number of people. Or, they are behind the scenes and we as humans have other recourse if the AI messes up. AI that is driving a car at 80 miles per hour on a highway had better not mess up. The consequences are grave. Multiply this by the number of cars, if we could put magically self-driving into every car in the USA, we'd have AI running in the 263 million cars. That's a lot of AI spread around. This is AI on a massive scale that we are not doing today and that offers both promise and potential peril.

There are some that want AI for self-driving cars because they envision a world without any car accidents. They envision a world in which there is no car congestion and all cars cooperate with each other. These are wonderful utopian visions.

They are also very misleading. The adoption of self-driving cars is going to be incremental and not overnight. We cannot economically just junk all existing cars. Nor are we going to be able to affordably retrofit existing cars. It is more likely that self-driving cars will be built into new cars and that over many years of gradual replacement of existing cars that we'll see the mix of self-driving cars become substantial in the real-world.

In these essays, I have tried to offer technological insights without being overly technical in my description, and also blended the business, societal, and economic aspects too. Technologists need to consider the non-technological impacts of what they do. Non-technologists should be aware of what is being developed.

We all need to work together to collectively be prepared for the enormous disruption and transformative aspects of true self-driving cars. We all need to be involved in this mother of all AI projects.

WHAT THIS BOOK PROVIDES

What does this book provide to you? It introduces many of the key elements about self-driving cars and does so with an AI based perspective. I weave together technical and non-technical aspects, readily going from being concerned about the cognitive capabilities of the driving task and how the technology is embodying this into self-driving cars, and in the next breath I discuss the societal and economic aspects.

They are all intertwined because that's the way reality is. You cannot separate out the technology per se, and instead must consider it within the milieu of what is being invented and innovated, and do so with a mindset towards the contemporary mores and culture that shape what we are doing and what we hope to do.

TOUR OF THIS BOOK

Let's do a quick tour of this book.

In Chapter 1, I take a look at genetic algorithms and indicate how they can be used for self-driving cars. In some ways, an esoteric realm of computer science, nonetheless genetic algorithms hold promise as an added innovative mathematical and computational method to improve AI for self-driving cars.

In Chapter 2, blockchain is discussed. Blockchain has become a darling of new technology and you might best know about it via the popularity of Bitcoins. Blockchain is a distributed database management system approach that has innovative promise for the AI of self-driving cars.

In Chapter 3, machine learning is an essential AI advancement that has helped to bring self-driving cars closer to reality. There is debate about the data that is needed for machine learning. I address this debate and offer thoughts on how it might be resolved.

In Chapter 4, there is an important discussion about so-called edge problems. This is a computer science term that refers to aspects considered not at the core of a problem being solved. Many in the self-driving car field believe that we can just put aside the known edge problems and deal with them later on. I say that the edge problems are at the core of a true self-driving car, and I provide hopefully compelling arguments in that favor.

In Chapter 5, I discuss one edge problem having to do with getting self-driving cars to be able to properly and safely navigate a roundabout (also known as a traffic circle or rotary).

In Chapter 6, I discuss another edge problem, parallel parking. Today's ability by self-driving cars to undertake parallel parking is nothing more than a simple parlor trick. We need to extend this parlor trick and develop some truly AI based parallel parking capabilities.

In Chapter 7, I share with you the emerging availability of open source software for self-driving cars. There are some that believe that self-driving software should be openly available to the public. Right now, most of the software is proprietary and guarded closely by the firms that are developing the AI systems.

In Chapter 8, the topic of cyber hacking of self-driving cars is covered. As you know, computer security is a big issue these days. We are constantly hearing about hacks into our bank accounts, our federal databases, and the like. The dangers of hacks done on self-driving cars involve life and death aspects. We need to have more attention to systems security for self-driving cars.

In Chapter 9, I discuss the edge problem of conspicuity. Our cars have ways to make themselves known to others around us, such as by the headlights, the horn, the emergency flashers, and so on. These should be utilized by self-driving cars too.

In Chapter 10, when a self-driving car comes upon an accident scene, what will it do? Right now, today's self-driving cars give up and hand control over to a human driver. We need to make self-driving cars able to be self-sufficient and handle accident scenes.

In Chapter 11, another edge problem involves dealing with emergency vehicles. Human drivers know that they are supposed to get out of the way of an emergency vehicle. Self-driving cars aren't yet being guided by AI to deal with this. It needs to happen.

In Chapter 12, left turns are bad, according to most statistics about car driving. Doing a left turn increases tremendously your risk of getting into an accident. Some think that self-driving cars should never make left turns. Read about my thoughts on this topic.

In Chapter 13, I discuss what happens when a sensor goes blind on a self-driving car. Right now, self-driving cars assume that their sensors are all working and will continue to properly work. This is not real-world. When you are in a self-driving car, the odds are that at some point the sensors will break or otherwise stop functioning. The AI needs to deal with this.

In Chapter 14, I discuss the edge problem of dealing with roadway debris. As human drivers, we know to watch out for and avoid debris that is on the roadway. Currently, most self-driving cars simply hand control over to a human driver. We need to have AI that understands what to do when confronted with roadway debris.

In Chapter 15, I discuss a very serious topic, pedestrian roadkill. By this I mean that if self-driving cars aren't better equipped and programmed, we are going to see pedestrians getting mowed down. This is ironic since everyone keeps claiming that self-driving cars will produce zero fatalities. Not true.

In Chapter 16, the topic of accidents is discussed. Self-driving cars are going to get into accidents. This might seem shocking. Aren't self-driving cars so clever that they will never get into an accident? I don't care how good a driver you are, if another car decides it is going to come at you at 80 miles per hour and ram into you, you will have little recourse if there is not sufficient time and space to avoid it.

In Chapter 17, there is a controversial topic that is worthy of discussion, namely that self-driving cars will need to drive illegally. How's that? Aren't self-driving cars going to always drive legally? No. There are circumstances wherein a self-driving car might need to drive illegally and we have to let the AI be aware of when to do so.

In Chapter 18, the topic of road signs is brought up. Some think that a self-driving car does not need to worry about road signs, because it presumably has a GPS capability. This is not very reassuring. There are many circumstances that involve driving and needing to read existing road signs in order to safely do the driving.

In Chapter 19, I cover aspects of parking a car. Similar to my parallel parking aspect, there are many other parking circumstances that need to be considered.

In Chapter 20, one of the most important and sobering topics is covered about self-driving cars. This has to do with the ability of human drivers to take over control from a self-driving car. There are serious issues underlying this notion.

In Chapter 21, I bring up the role of government and regulators as it applies to self-driving cars. Should there be no regulations covering self-driving cars? Should there be heavy regulatory action? These are questions that we need to all consider.

In Chapter 22, there is an edge problem that I refer to as the head nod. When we are driving, we see other humans and interpret what they are doing and intend to do by looking at their body language. This is not being done by today's self-driving cars. We need to add this into the AI for self-driving cars.

In Chapter 23, I have included an essay about self-driving cars that I wrote while attending the Consumer Electronics Show (CES) in 2017. Though this will quickly become further and further dated, I include the piece to emphasize that all self-driving cars are different, and that each vendor is taking their own particular approach to what they believe a self-driving car is and should do.

WHY THIS BOOK

I wrote this book to try and bring to the public view many aspects about self-driving cars that nobody seems to be discussing.

For business leaders that are either involved in making self-driving cars or that are going to leverage self-driving cars, I hope that this book will enlighten you as to the risks involved and ways in which you should be strategizing about how to deal with those risks.

For entrepreneurs, startups and other businesses that want to enter into the self-driving car market that is emerging, I hope this book sparks your interest in doing so, and provides some sense of what might be prudent to pursue.

For researchers that study self-driving cars, I hope this book spurs your interest in the risks and safety issues of self-driving cars, and also nudges you toward conducting research on those aspects.

For students in computer science or related disciplines, I hope this book will provide you with interesting and new ideas and material, for which you might conduct research or provide some career direction insights for you.

For AI companies and high-tech companies pursuing self-driving cars, this book will hopefully broaden your view beyond just the mere coding and development needed to make self-driving cars.

For all readers, I hope that you will find the material in this book to be stimulating. Some of it will be repetitive of things you already know. But I am pretty sure that you'll also find various eureka moments whereby you'll discover a new technique or approach that you had not earlier thought of. I am also betting that there will be material that forces you to rethink some of your current practices.

I am not saying you will suddenly have an epiphany and change what you are doing. I do think though that you will reconsider or perhaps revisit what you are doing.

For anyone choosing to use this book for teaching purposes, please take a look at my suggestions for doing so, as described in the Appendix. I have found the material handy in courses that I have taught, and likewise other faculty have told me that they have found the material handy, in some cases as extended readings and in other instances as a core part of their course (depending on the nature of the class).

In my writing for this book, I have tried carefully to blend both the practitioner and the academic styles of writing. It is not as dense as is typical academic journal writing, but at the same time offers depth by going into the nuances and trade-offs of various practices.

The word "deep" is in vogue today, meaning getting deeply into a subject or topic, and so is the word "unpack" which means to tease out the underlying aspects of a subject or topic. I have sought to offer material that addresses an issue or topic by going relatively deeply into it and make sure that it is well unpacked.

Finally, in any book about AI, it is difficult to use our everyday words without having some of them be misinterpreted. Specifically, it is easy to anthropomorphize AI. When I say that an AI system "knows" something, I do not want you to construe that the AI system has sentience and "knows" in the same way that humans do. They aren't that way, as yet. I have tried to use quotes around such words from time-to-time to emphasize that the words I am using should not be misinterpreted to ascribe true human intelligence to the AI systems that we know of today. If I used quotes around all such words, the book would be very difficult to read, and so I am doing so judiciously. Please keep that in mind as you read the material, thanks.

COMPANION BOOK

If you find this material of interest, you might want to also see my other book on self-driving cars, entitled ***Self-Driving Cars: "The Mother of ALL AI Projects"*** and contains more of my at-times controversial and under-the-hood explorations about the nature of self-driving cars.

CHAPTER 1

GENETIC ALGORTHIMS FOR SELF-DRIVING CARS

Lance B. Eliot

CHAPTER 1

GENETIC ALGORTHIMS FOR SELF-DRIVING CARS

I was watching the National Geographic cable channel the other day and marveled at a type of leopard that could leap several feet into the air to catch a bird mid-flight.

The leopard at first had tried to get the bird while the bird was on the ground, but the bird was wise to the approaching leopard and opted to scurry into the air to get away. Seemed like the bird launching into the air would have been more than sufficient to escape the ground-based prowling leopard. But, the leopard had anticipated that the bird would try to fly away, and cleverly the leopard ran at an angle that coincided with the upward trajectory of the bird, and managed to leap several feet into the air to intersect with the bird as it was taking off.

A few more seconds and the bird would have reached a height that the leopard could not have achieved. Upon reflection of this leopard's behavior, you need to really admire the physics aspects of the leopard being able to calculate the proper angle, speed, timing, and direction when it made its leap, since it was able to precisely snatch the bird in mid-stride and bring it down to the ground. Score that as one win for the leopard family (another meal), one loss for the bird family.

How did the leopard know to make the leap? Did it go to college and learn it in school? Is there some kind of "leopard hunting" manual that the leopard had been reading? Those seem like unlikely explanations. A more plausible explanation would be that this type of leopard is the product of biological evolution. Over time, leopards that were able to ascertain how to best leap into the air to catch birds were presumably more likely to survive. Those leopards that were unable to add this tactic to their capabilities or that were not prone to it were less likely to get meals, and so they tended to starve off and not be around to reproduce. Leopards that inherited the ability to make these leaps were more likely to get meals, and more likely to survive, and thus more likely to reproduce. Eventually, leopards with this trait won out and become populous, while the leopards that did not have this trait lost out and became extinct.

There's a well-known name for this explanation. Darwinism. As we all know today, Charles Darwin proposed a theory of evolution, which was published in 1859 in his now classic book "On the Origin of Species," and for which his theory has gained widespread acceptance. His focus was on species of organisms and how natural selection leads to those that survive versus those that do not survive. In many ways, this theory was controversial when first proposed. Even today, there are some critics that don't completely buy into his theory. There are also ongoing debates about what his theory implies about the fundamental nature of mankind and creation. I'm not going to open that Pandora's box here.

I was reminded of Darwinism this morning while driving to work. A colleague was in my car and we were slogging through the dreadful bumper-to-bumper morning freeway traffic. We were both visually scanning the traffic scene for any opportunity to somehow get ahead in the traffic. Suddenly, a car that was in the carpool lane made a mad dash out of the carpool lane. It illegally crossed the double-yellow lines that mark-off the carpool lane (see my article about self-driving cars and illegal driving), and then this same pushy car cut through all four other lanes of traffic. The driver was evidently trying to make a freeway exit but had not planned well to get to it. Besides cutting across all lanes and causing cars to abruptly slam on their brakes, he also just barely made the off-ramp. He actually knocked over some cones at the off-ramp due to his wild maneuver and had been not able to get properly aligned to make the exit safely.

My colleague and I were stunned at the reckless and brazen act of the wanton driver. We both looked at each other and in the same moment said "Darwinism," which was our way of conveying that we figured that his kind would ultimately get crushed or killed in a car accident, and he would eventually be weeding his kind out of the population pool. Of course, we didn't actually believe this per se, it was more a figure of speech and bit of humor to lighten the stressful moment, but it highlights how much Darwin's theories have permeated our everyday efforts and thoughts.

There is a line of inquiry and study that has tried to use Darwin's theories for the development of mathematical algorithms development and for use in developing computer systems. This field of study is known as genetic algorithms. Basically, they are step-by-step procedures that try to use the same concepts that underlie the theory of evolution. Be aware that there are various competing ways in which these genetic algorithms work, and there is no one specific standard per se. Different researchers and computer scientists have opted to implement genetic algorithms in varying ways. Generally, the overall approach is the same, but if you decide to use a specific software package or write your own software code, keep in mind that your use of genetic algorithms might differ from someone else's use.

At the Cybernetic Self-Driving Car lab, we have been using genetic algorithms in ways that help self-driving cars.

Genetic algorithms can be used for standalone purposes, they can be used by embedding them into the self-driving car AI capabilities, and they can be used in conjunction with neural networks and other machine learning mechanisms (see my article about machine learning and self-driving cars). In this article, I'll describe some ways in which we are using genetic algorithms for advancing self-driving cars.

Let's start my example of genetic algorithms by bringing up an ongoing friendly debate between me and my daughter. As driver, she likes to really put the peddle to the metal. Every time she drivers her car, it is like an Indy race that involves her going as fast as possible, cutting all corners, and clawing for any means to reduce her travel time and get to her destination the soonest possible. In contrast, I am the perhaps stereotypical fatherly driving driver, namely I stop fully at all stop signs, I don't gun the engine, I seek to get to my destination as soon as practical but with safety as a key factor in my approach. My daughter believes that my style of driving is archaic and over-the-hill, and furthermore that her style of driving is modern, realistic, and the only way to expeditiously get to any destination. All I can say is that the number of dings, scratches, and other bumps on her car are suggestive that her approach, though maybe indeed more expeditious, also has the potential for some really adverse consequences.

My team at the Cybernetics Self-Driving Lab has overheard (ad nauseam) the lighthearted debates that me and my daughter have about driving styles. Over and over, I claim that I can pretty much get to the same destination as she, with marginal difference in time expended, and yet in a much safer manner. She claims that my style would add a huge amount of time to any driving excursion. Who is right? Intuitively, I realize that it seems logical that she must be right in that certainly if you go as fast as possible you would reach your destination sooner than someone else. But, I claim that this intuitive notion is actually false when you include certain kinds of traffic conditions.

If there is heavy traffic on the roads, you are going to be bound by their progress. During my morning commute on the freeway, I see cars that try to go as fast as they can, but they get locked into the rest of traffic and so their attempts at going fast are blunted. Yes, they might accelerate very quickly in little pockets or gaps of traffic, but nonetheless the rest of traffic is still keeping them going at a measured pace. Speed-up, slow down, speed-up slow down, this is the outcome of a frantic speeder driving style in those traffic conditions. I assert that a more paced driver would be able to make the same amount of progress, and yet not be doing the useful speed-up's and slowdowns that the frantic driver is doing.

A means to characterize this debate is to consider it as an optimization problem. We want to optimize the time it takes to get to a destination X, doing so in heavy traffic conditions T, and use some set of driving techniques S, in order to ascertain which is the "best" solution. To make this a fair fight, we would want to keep the T approximately equivalent for any comparison of the set S. So, the set S of driving techniques might be a really good solution for light traffic conditions (a lite T), but then not be very good in heavy traffic conditions (a busy T). This is important in that my daughter's style might be a tremendous solution when driving on the open road for miles and miles, since there are no obstructions and therefore going fast is in fact going to be the soonest arrival. On the other hand, when freeway traffic is solid and you can't get going fast anyway, her solution might be equal to or maybe even worse than mine.

The team at the Cybernetics Self-Driving Car Lab decided to go ahead and use a genetic algorithm to test out the competing approaches to driving style. A genetic algorithm uses Darwinian aspects to try and solve an optimization problem. Besides trying to settle the debate that my daughter and I are having, it is useful for self-driving cars too, since the question rightfully arises as to what kind of style of driving a self-driving car should have.

Most of self-driving car makers are assuming that the AI of a self-driving car should always be the most legal and most slow-poke kind of driver. This is sufficient right now during the research and development stages of self-driving cars. Once self-driving cars are truly in the real-world, we are likely to see that human occupants will want their self-driving car to be more aggressive. Some human buyers of self-driving cars might even use as a criterion of which self-driving car to buy whether it is one that is the "old granny" style driving or whether it can accommodate the "race car" driver style. I have been saying that self-driving car makers need to provide multiple driving styles and allow the human to select which kind of ride they want. Right now, self-driving car makers are making it as "one style fits all" and we'll likely gradually see the marketplace want choices. That's why we are developing the multiple styles at our Cybernetics Self-Driving Car Lab, in anticipation of a gradual realization that it is what humans will want to have their self-driving car be able to do.

Let's get back to the genetic algorithm aspects. Typically, you start by creating a random initial population shaped around whatever structure you've decided upon. In this case, we defined that a driving style consists of these factors:

- Speed Style
- Lane Changing Style
- Braking Style
- Distances Style
- Risk Style

This small set of factors is sufficient for a rudimentary setup, and there are added factors in our more robust version.

For the Speed Style, we established that you can be a very "fast going" driver, or instead be a more measured driver. For the Lane Changing Style, we established that you can be a continually lane changing driver, or instead an infrequent lane changer. For Braking

Style, we used whether you are a hard-braking driver that comes to abrupt stops and rides your brakes, or instead you are a driver that uses the brakes only when necessary. For the factor on Distances Style, we established that you are a driver that drives right up to the butt of another car, or instead one that allows for appropriate stopping distances between cars. For the Risk Style, we established that you are a high-risk driver that cuts things closely and takes significant chances of getting into a car accident, or instead you are lower risk driver that seeks to ensure safety as you drive.

Each of these factors is not a black-and-white scale per se, but instead more akin to a slider scale of being toward one end of the spectrum versus the other end. You don't have to be only a completely go-fast driver and nor only just a go-slow driver, you can be somewhere in-between.

The nature of the trip itself is a crucial aspect. Just as in Darwinism, the environment is what determines fitness. If the leopard was in an environment where there weren't any birds, it would be unlikely that the leopards that had a leaping capability would be a better fit over other leopards, and so that jumping trait would not be rewarded by being able to get more meals. For this self-driving car example, we opted to do my normal daily commute, which takes me anywhere from ninety minutes to two hours in very heavy morning freeway traffic conditions. We also have collected actual traffic data that indicates the patterns of cars that are in the morning traffic, such as how many cars there are, their driving behaviors, and so on.

Let's then suppose that we are trying to figure out that in this defined T, we will use a driving approach S that consists of the driving style of my daughter, and the goal is to minimize the time it takes to get the destination X where I work, and do so with the least number of accidents. It is important to include in the optimization that the least number of accidents is a factor, since without it you could potentially bump into other cars and opt to just proceed ahead, but this is not realistic and getting into accidents should be a penalty.

On any given single trip of making the commute, one driving style might turn out more optimal than the other, due to variances, and so we need to simulate the trip numerous times to gauge whether the driving style is overall optimal or not (see my article about simulations and self-driving cars). We ran this simulation for thousands of trips. This is equivalent to realizing that Darwinism tends to take many years of evolution to see changes appear, and it is not something that tends to happen in the near-term. We also opted to divide the driving into segments, and adjust the driving style at each segment.

Using my daughter's driving style, we created a population of drivers with her aggressiveness. We scored each member of the population based on their fitness score. This is considered the "current" population and is used to create the next generation. Essentially, these are the parents which will contribute their genes toward their children.

For the next generation of the population, there are three kinds of children as based on the current population:

- Elite children are those with the best fitness value from the current population and so are considered to survive to the next generation.

- Crossover children are created by crossing genes from two parents and producing a child with a mix of their characteristics.

- Mutation children are created by mutations or random changes made to a selected parent.

At each driving segment, we took what was the current population, in this case aggressive drivers like my daughter, and produced offspring of having a tendency toward aggressive driving (which becomes the next generation). Some of the offspring would be just like the current population (elites), some of the offspring were a mix of two parents from the current population (crossovers), and some of the offspring were different from the current population (having been mutated).

Using the leopard analogy, go back in time before there were leaping leopards. At first, let's assume leopards didn't particularly leap. For that "current" population, they reproduced to generate their next generation of leopards. We could just assume that all leopards produced as offspring are identical to the current population, and so the current population becomes the next generation, but that's not what happens according to Darwin.

Instead, though there are some offspring that are identical to a single parent (elites). But, there are also some offspring that are based on a combination from their parents (crossovers), which if you have had children you probably noticed in your own children that they seem to be a mixture of both the father and the mother in ways that makes them unique in comparison to their parents (in other words, the child exhibits some traits that the mother has but the father does not, and traits that the father has that the mother does not).

There is also the mutation aspect. Sometimes a child seems to have a trait that neither the mother and nor the father seem to have. Nature seems to introduce random variation that can presumably lead to offspring that will have a better chance at fitness, beyond what their parents had. In this case of the self-driving car, we allowed that the aggressive driver traits could be mutated, for example that the hard braking of an aggressive driver, which normally carries into the next generation or offspring, could have a random mutation that made it no longer a hard braking but maybe a softer braking.

After having setup the genetic algorithm for this, we ran it. You can run it based on how many times you want it to run, or there are other limits you can set, such as so-called "stalls" which is a measure of how far the next generation is from the current generation (if subsequent generations are not changing much, it probably suggests you can stop running the genetic algorithm). The runs can be allowed to go indefinitely and instead the focus be on the fitness test, in essence saying run this until the algorithm has reached a certain fitness point.

The results were fascinating.

In the end, in terms of greatest fitness and optimization, the aggressive style morphed towards a more moderate style. This appeared to support my contention that when faced with heavy traffic conditions over a somewhat lengthy path, the purist aggressiveness style does not in the long-run gain you much advantage and that instead a more moderate driving style is "better" for such conditions. My daughter isn't going to change her driving behavior because of this, and she genuinely enjoys her aggressive driving style, plus her style might well be better in shorter trips (we need to test this!), so the genetic algorithm effort that we did won't be impacting her.

We believe though that this kind of use of genetic algorithms is important for self-driving cars and how the AI proceeds.

Using genetic algorithms for self-driving cars is likely done outside the actual driving of the car. It is more akin to a design technique to assess differing ways to have the AI drive the car. Trying to use a genetic algorithm while in the midst of the AI driving a car is not only computationally intensive and expensive, it is questionable whether you would want to immediately put into play the outcome of the genetic algorithm without some other inspection of what it had produced.

Genetic algorithms can though potentially be used by sensor fusion for a self-driving car, which can be done beforehand (prior to embedding sensor fusion into the self-driving car), or could possibly done in real-time. This would allow you for example to determine LIDAR data in real-time (see my article about LIDAR) or camera images and video streams.

One increasingly useful aspect for genetic algorithms has been to tune neural networks. When you setup a neural network, there are various parameters that you need to establish. How do we know what will be a good setting for those parameters? A means to figure that out involves using a genetic algorithm that runs many generations of those parameters and tries to identify via a fitness function which settings will be the "best" or optimal for the neural network.

Genetic algorithms are at the far edge of the self-driving car industry and not yet being especially utilized by the self-driving car makers. We will gradually see this algorithmic technique shift from being mainly research oriented and become more real-world used by the self-driving car makers. It is another tool in the toolkit for self-driving car makers. And, the more you want to push a self-driving car toward the level 5 (see my article about the Richter scale for self-driving cars), you'll need to bring to the forefront any advanced tool that can help make that leap to a true self-driving car.

.

CHAPTER 2

BLOCKCHAIN FOR SELF-DRIVING CARS

CHAPTER 2

BLOCKCHAIN FOR
SELF-DRIVING CARS

f you've heard anything at all about "blockchain" it probably would be the voluminous and breathless exclamations that it is a disruptive innovation that will change society and the world. It is one of the hottest emerging technologies and as is usually the case with something "new and hot" has garnered some fanatical fans. Or, you might vaguely be aware that blockchain somehow relates to bitcoins. You are likely to have seen or heard that bitcoins are some kind of curious new currency that is available in the online realm. You might be unsure about bitcoins, whether they are trustworthy or not, and whether to maybe get yourself some bitcoins or let the whole thing shake out first. Seems like blockchain and also bitcoins are in the midst of the unsettled, wild-wild-west of technology that maybe or maybe not will eventually calm down into something beyond those that are at the fringe of high-tech. Let's go through the fundamentals of what this is all about, and then take a serious look at what this has to do with self-driving cars.

At the Cybernetics Self-Driving Cars Lab, we are making use of blockchains for self-driving cars. We are exploring and proving out the mettle of blockchain.

We are not the only ones integrating blockchain and self-driving cars as there is interest on this topic by others in the self-driving car industry. Indeed, a recent announcement by the Toyota Research Institute (TRI) illustrates the intense interest in figuring out how to best exploit blockchains for self-driving cars. TRI announced that they are "exploring blockchain and distributed ledger technology (BC/DL) for use in the development of a new mobility ecosystem that could accelerate development of autonomous driving technology." Partnering up with MIT's Media Lab, TRI has also indicated they are working with several start-up's including BigChainDB, Oaken Innovation, CommuterZ, and Gem.

Let's start at the beginning. What is blockchain? What are bitcoins? I'll first explain what blockchain is. Then, we'll discuss bitcoins.

Simply stated, blockchain is a distributed database, meaning that it is just like a normal database that you are already used to except that it is setup to have lots of copies of the database that are floating around among many computers in a distributed manner. I might put my database on a hundred different computers around the world and ask them all to keep it handy in case I need to access it. This is convenient for me because it ensures that my database is redundant and so if somehow one of those computers loses it that I could go to another one that still has it and be able to get access to my database.

You might be wondering whether I am worried that my database which is distributed all around the world will be seen by others and they could read whatever is in my database. I would in fact be concerned about that. Thus, another aspect of blockchain is that the distributed database is encrypted. Using data security aspects, the database is encrypted and only with the proper keys can anyone actually read it.

Okay, so far, we are agreed that blockchain is a distributed database, in which my data is placed at perhaps hundreds or even thousands of computers all around the world. It has redundancy because of this. It also is encrypted so that only someone with the proper encryption keys can actually read it. You might next be wondering how could I make changes to the database, assuming that I wanted to say add some further data to the database. If I do so, how would I make sure that all hundreds or thousands of the copies of my database are equally updated. I don't want to end-up in a situation where some of those copies of my database are outdated and other copies are updated. This would certainly be confusing because then I wouldn't know which copy of the database is accurate.

The way in which changes to the database are handled involves the aspect that the database has already been subdivided into what are called blocks, essentially chunks of data. When I want to add more data to my database, I add another block to it. Suppose that my database already has five blocks of data, and those five blocks (considered collected together and intact as my current database) are distributed across hundreds or thousands of computers, and I decide that I want to add more data. I would place a new block into one copy of database and ask all the others that have a copy of my database to likewise add that new block to their copy. This request would promulgate across a wide network connecting those computers and one-by-one each of them that has a copy of my database would add the new block to it. This might seem like it would take a while to do, but in normal everyday aspects it can be relatively fast, depending upon the speeds of the computers and the speed of the network.

Voila, we now are to a juncture of this discussion to point out that this approach is called "blockchain" and this is due to the aspect that the database is composed of a series of blocks of data, and furthermore they are "chained" together. Let me explain the chaining aspect. For my database which now has six blocks, the newest block that I had just added has a link to the fifth block. The fifth block already has a link to the fourth block. The fourth block links to the third block, the third block links to the second block, and the second block links to the first block. All the blocks of the database have a link, of which, the link in the latest block links to the block that preceded it. They are like a chain, with each block being connected to each other in a linear, serial way.

Linking together the blocks is helpful to make sure that you can always find all the blocks of the database, though realize that you can only figure out the other blocks that preceded whichever block you are looking at. If I look at the sixth block, I can traverse all the way to the first block. But, if I am looking only at the third block, say, it links just to the second block and the first block. So, when I get ahold of a copy of my database, I would want to start with the latest block in order to walk back through all other blocks.

Each block usually has a timestamp that indicates the date and time when it was added to the database. It also has a special encryption-like "hash" code that helps to make sure that it is legitimately part of my database. The hash code for block six is based on the hash code of block five, and block five's hash code is based on block four, and so on. Here's why this is helpful. If someone decided to change block four of my database, they would end-up changing the hash code too (there are mathematical technical aspects of why this would occur). Any other computer that received this version of the database would be able to realize that someone has changed something in my database, which is not allowed to happen. Once a block has been accepted into a blockchain database, it must never be changed. It will stay the same.

As recap so far, blockchain is a distributed database, having lots of copies spread on computers potentially across the globe, and the database consists of blocks of data that are chained together from the latest to the earliest of the blocks. Furthermore, the blocks cannot be changed, you can only add new blocks to the database. When a new block is added to a copy of the database, it is linked to the topmost block to-date, plus it uses a special hash code that numerically uniquely identifies it and will essentially allow the "prevention" (detection) of later changes being made that could otherwise happen undetected.

I am sure you love arcane terminology, so let's include some here.

The computers that are willing to hang onto a copy of my database are often referred to as "nodes" (in a moment, when discussing bitcoins, the "nodes" are referred to as miners). My database grows in height when I add new blocks to it (we refer to the size of the database as its height, in a sense it grows taller as I add blocks to it). Due to cleverly using the hash encoding as an integral aspect of blockchain, the database is considered "immutable" because if anyone tampers with any of the blocks to try and change them then mathematically it can be ascertained that something is amiss and the copy of the database that someone messed with can be rejected as being an invalid copy. It is "auditable" because we can inspect the blocks links to ensure that it is all intact and essentially a single-source-of-truth and know how and when the blocks were added to the database. The way in which the computers communicate to each other about the distributed databases is done on a peer-to-peer (P2P) basis, meaning that one computer talks to another one, and they share back-and-forth what's going on with the databases.

Presumably, the blockchain approach provides for a database that is secure and private, since it is encrypted and requires permission to read it. The cryptographic techniques and the data partitioning into blocks allows me to selectively allow others to have visibility into the database. In near real-time the database can be updated, depending upon the speed of the network and the computers involved. Some would say that the blockchain then is a distributed database that is sustainable, secure, private, immutable, shared, and computationally trustworthy.

Blockchain then is an overarching approach to enacting a distributed database. It is not any specific technology per se, but instead an approach consisting of techniques and algorithms. Anyone that wants to put together a blockchain can do so. There is software that allows you to setup a blockchain. You could even write code to create your own blockchain.

There are public instances of blockchains, and there are private instances of blockchains. For a private blockchain, I might arrange with firms in say the insurance industry that want to share data with each other and then setup a blockchain that is just for them. Only they would have access to the network and computers that house the blockchain that they are using. For a public blockchain, the blockchain or distributed databases would be on publicly available computers, typically housed across the open Internet.

You can think of the blockchain as something that you would use to build an application for (hopefully) some useful purpose. Like I just mentioned, if a bunch of insurance companies wanted to share data with each other, I could create an "application" of blockchain that was just for them. In a sense, some people like to think of blockchain as the operating system or platform and then you build applications on top of it.

One of the most famous of all applications that uses blockchain is bitcoins.

Bitcoins are an instantiation of blockchain. This makes sense when you give it a moment to sink in. If you wanted to create a new currency, how would you do so? If you were to go the paper route and printed paper money, it would be pretty expensive to print up that paper money and make sure it was tamper proof. We've seen how hard the U.S. Treasury Department works to make sure our dollar bills are tamper proof, which otherwise we'd have lots of fraudulent money floating around. Well, if you wanted to make a new currency, you'd be nuts to try and make it paper-based since it is so expensive to print it and make sure it is tamper proof. Plus, getting that paper money physically to all parts of the world to be used as a global currency is going to tough to do and expensive to spread around.

Instead, in today's world, you'd make that new currency be all digital. It would simply be online and you would want some means to record the amounts and the transactions. You'd want it to be accessed anywhere in the world. You'd want it to be accessed pretty much instantaneously. You'd want it to be secure. Voila, which is the second time I've said voila in this piece, if you wanted to create a new currency you would want some kind of underlying platform or operating system upon which to build it that could do all these things. Answer: blockchain.

Bitcoins are an imaginary currency that exists by having people agree that this thing we agree to be a type of currency and that is recorded via blockchain is actually worth value of some kind. Blockchain ecomes the means to record the bitcoin transactions. You give me some bitcoins, and someone else gives you some bitcoins, and this is all recorded into a database, allowing us to know who has what number of bitcoins. What powers bitcoins is the use of blockchain, which provides the foundation or platform for ensuring a distributed database of ledger transactions. The ledger is secure, distributed, immutable, etc., due to making use of blockchain underneath.

We'll add some more terminology to this. Bitcoins are considered a type of cryptocurrency. That's big speak for virtual money that is kept online and encrypted. Once bitcoin made a splash, others realized that they could also use blockchain and try to promote alternative made-up currencies. In essence, anyone, including you, can start your own online currency, if you wish to do so, merely by making use of blockchain. You could call it "LanceCoin" (I like the sound of that!), or ItsyBitsyCoin, or SuperCurrency, or whatever.

Now, that being said, you'd need to try and convince other people that your made-up currency is something that has value and that they should be willing to use it. Right now, bitcoin has the most momentum of the cryptocurrencies. It is kind of like Facebook, in that when Facebook first got rolling there were other competing social media apps like it, but it seemed to garner the most attraction and eventually steamrolled past its competitors. Bitcoin has that kind of momentum, but the jury is still out whether it will take hold, and/or whether something else might arise that knocks it from its high perch.

One aspect of blockchain that I didn't explicitly point out that you might have anyway realized is that there is no one master keeper of the database. Usually, we are used to have someone or something that keeps a master database and everyone else goes to that single master copy to know what's the latest data of the database. Blockchain is a technique that eliminates the need for a single master keeper of the database. We say that there isn't an "intermediary" needed to maintain the database. Instead, its maintenance is distributed and no one in particular owns it.

This is both the advantage and disadvantage facing a cryptocurrency such as bitcoin. Bitcoin touts that it is not controlled by anyone in particular. We know that U.S. dollars are controlled by the United States government, and that likewise most currencies are controlled by either a particular country or by a group of countries such as the EU. Bitcoin is not based on any particular country or group to back it. It is based solely on what many would say is self-interests. It is considered a mass collaboration.

If you believe that currency when backed by a particular country or group is a form of tyranny, you then really like bitcoins and cryptocurrency because it is freer, it is a democratization of currency, some suggest. For most people, the idea of a currency which is not backed by any particular country or group seems highly questionable and speculative. Thus, though bitcoin touts its freedoms aspects, this same aspect can be quite unnerving to others and so they are hesitant to make use of cryptocurrencies.

You can now award yourself a certificate of awareness of what blockchain is, and what bitcoin is. Congratulations! But, I realize that you started reading this due to wanting to know how blockchain applies to self-driving cars. I didn't forget, and just wanted to get you to a level playing field of what blockchain is all about.

One way in which blockchain applies to self-driving cars is regarding driving data. In my writings contained in this book, such as my indication of machine learning and self-driving cars, I mentioned that there is the potential of wanting to keep track of driving data that is recorded by self-driving cars. We will ultimately have presumably the roadways filled with self-driving cars, and those self-driving cars are chock full of sensors that record visual images and video via cameras, they can record distance data via radar sensors, LIDAR data and so on.

Some believe that the data of these self-driving cars should be shared so as to be able to analyze the data and improve the AI of self-driving cars. Imagine how massive that data would be. You could use machine learning to cull that data and try to improve self-driving cars ability to drive. But, this also raises privacy issues. Are you ok that your self-driving car is telling all about where you went, when you went there, etc.? Privacy proponents are very concerned that allowing the collection and sharing of the self-driving car sensor data will bring forth Big Brother.

A proposed solution would be to allow self-driving car data to go into a blockchain that then you could personally decide to whom you would allow your data to be used. Your data would be preserved in the blockchain, but not automatically readable. You could decide whom can access it. You might even get paid by someone to allow access, such as a self-driving car maker might pay you to let them access your driving data. Or, maybe companies that want to know patterns of consumers behavior as to where they go and when they go there, would pay you. Or, maybe Wal-Mart or other retailers might pay you, since they would want to know whether you drive near their stores and what they could then do to get you to stop at their stores.

I am asked why we can't already do this today. I point out that the main stoppage is that few cars have the sensors needed to collect the driving data, and also few cars have the Internet connectivity to transmit the data into a blockchain. Though, there are some cars that are already doing this in a smaller way. The car insurance company Progressive is known for their Snapshot tool, which plugs into the diagnostic port of your car, and then provides aspects of your driving data to them. This is a usage-based insurance (UBI) program, claiming to reward good drivers by knowing what kind of driving they do. When we have self-driving cars aplenty, those self-driving cars will have lots of sensors and lots of data, and will already be built with Internet connectivity, and so the data sharing aspects will be much easier and become a more popular topic of debate and discussion.

Speaking of car insurance, we don't yet know how car insurance will be handled in a world of self-driving cars, but anyway assuming there is some form of car insurance, you could use blockchain to do usage-based insurance, or even pay as you drive (PAYD) insurance. PAYD is where you pay for car insurance in increments of perhaps five minutes, and it is based on where you are driving (safe areas versus dangerous areas), when you are driving (daytime versus nighttime), etc. If your driving data of your self-driving car is being fed into a blockchain, it would be pretty easy to allow an insurance company to then offer you PAYD or UBI.

Another aspect of using blockchain for self-driving cars involves Shared Autonomous Vehicles (SAV). Right now, when you want to get a car akin to a taxi, you probably are using Uber or Lyft, or some similar ride sharing service. When we have self-driving cars, the question arises as to what you will do with your self-driving car while you are at work or asleep. Currently, your car sits and does nothing, somewhat like a horse in the barn waiting for you to want to go for a ride (some estimates indicate that you only use your car currently for perhaps 5-10% of the day!). Instead, suppose you put that horse to other uses, in other words you allowed your self-driving car to be used by others. You become your own version of Uber or Lyft.

Uber and Lyft are going to pitch to you that you should join into their online network so as to allow people that want rides to even know that your self-driving car is available for ride sharing. Of course, Uber or Lyft will take a cut of whatever you charge the persons that use your self-driving car. Facebook, meanwhile, figures why would you use Uber or Lyft for that purpose and instead you could just post onto Facebook that your car is available for ride sharing. It's going to be an ugly battle for eyeballs.

Some say forget entirely about Uber, Lyft, Facebook, and all those others, and instead use blockchain (this is really, really scary to the execs at Uber, Lyft, and any other ride sharing service!). A public blockchain could be crafted and it would allow for those that want to take rides to find out who is offering their self-driving car for rides. Guess what, no intermediary! No Uber needed, no Lyft needed, etc. No cutting them into the fees you are charging for the use of your self-driving car. With the touch of a button, you can add your car to a publicly available blockchain that represents fleets of cars all throughout the world.

Another use of blockchain for self-driving cars involves currency. You take your self-driving car to the car wash, and instead of paying via cash or credit card, instead you use an online currency like bitcoin or something else that has come along. You could do that today, but it is a hassle. Once we have self-driving cars, and with their Internet connectivity, it would be pretty easy for them to also do the online transactions that apply to your self-driving car. If you drive through a McDonald's or Taco Bell, your self-driving car could pay for the transaction, via a blockchain that those fast-food eateries have agreed to use. This scares the heck out of Visa, American Express, and all other credit card companies.

Is blockchain then the answer to all our problems? Is it the silver bullet? No. It is a type of distributed database that has properties that make it amenable for interesting societal and business aspects, and will gradually become further popularized as we continue to push toward a digital world, and especially so with self-driving cars because we are essentially going digital in many ways far beyond what our cars do today. Self-driving cars will be chock full of sensors, processors, and be online, all of which then means they are increasingly becoming digitalized and we ought to be considering ways in which we can leverage those digital-based capabilities.

We must also consider the underbelly of blockchain. The way it works now, data does not go away in a blockchain. It always exists. This has important privacy considerations and we aren't used to the idea that data about you is always around. For those using Facebook, and getting older, they are beginning to regret that they posted stuff onto Facebook when they were younger and for which now exists elsewhere because others might have grabbed it up at the time. We have generally been living in a society where data eventually decays, becomes lost to the ages. Can we handle an era of data that never goes away?

There is also the opportunity for exploitation and hacking of blockchain. It is all based on cryptographic techniques that we consider hard to crack. Maybe there are holes in those algorithms and we just don't yet know it. Maybe the software that enacts it has bugs in it. By the way, most of the encryption algorithms are based on the idea that you could crack it but that it isn't feasible given the tremendous mathematical and computational effort it would take to break it. As the availability of computer processing continues to escalate, and the cost of computations decreases, we might find ways to realistically crack these puzzles. Indeed, quantum computing offers orders of magnitude increases in speed of computations.

Blockchain is one of the latest and hottest buzzwords. There is no magic in it. Think of it as souped-up cryptographic distributed database that we can use as a platform for creating useful applications. Besides useful applications like cryptocurrency, of which bitcoin is the most notable, we can use it for other kinds of public and also private applications. This can also be used for nefarious purposes, such as an international crime ring that wants to share their illicit efforts and do so via the Internet, right in front of everyone's eyes, which might seem like a wild idea, but with the right kind of approach they could potentially pull it off. Anyway, for self-driving cars, there are lots of ways that the advent of digitalizing the car will play into using blockchain applications, such as online payments for services, getting on-the-spot car insurance, and for the possible sharing of driving data. Drive safe other there!

.

CHAPTER 3

MACHINE LEARNING AND DATA
FOR SELF-DRIVING CARS

CHAPTER 3

MACHINE LEARNING AND DATA FOR SELF-DRIVING CARS

The crux of any machine learning approach involves data. You need lots and lots of usable data to be able to "teach" a machine. One of the reasons that machine learning has progressed lately is due to the advent of Big Data, meaning tons of data that can be readily captured, stored, and processed. Why is there a necessity to have an abundance of data for purposes of doing machine learning? Let's use a simple but illustrative example to explain this. Imagine if you wanted to learn about birds and someone showed you only one individual picture of a bird (and furthermore, let's assume you had never seen any birds in your lifetime). It might be difficult to generalize from one picture and discern the actual characteristics of a bird. If you saw perhaps 50 pictures you'd have a greater chance of discovering that birds have wings, they have beaks, etc. If you saw thousands and thousands of pictures of birds you'd be able to really begin to figure out their characteristics, and even be able to classify birds by aspects such as distinctive colors, distinctive wing shapes, and so on.

For self-driving cars, many of the self-driving car makers are utilizing machine learning to imbue their AI systems with an ability to drive a car. What kind of data are the developers using to "teach" the automation to drive a car? The developers are capturing huge amounts of data that arises while a car is being driven, collecting the data from a myriad of sensors on the car. These sensors include cameras that are capturing images and video, radar devices that capture radar signals, LIDAR devices that capture laser-based distance points data, and the like. All of this data can be fed into a massive dataset, and then

43

crunched and processed by machine learning algorithms. Indeed, Tesla does this data collection over-the-air from their Tesla cars and can enhance their existing driving algorithms by examining the data and using it to learn new aspects about how their Autopilot software can improve as a driver of the car.

How much data are we talking about?

One estimate by Intel is the following:

- Radar data: 10 to 100 KB per second

- Camera data: 20 to 40 MB per second

- Sonar data: 10 to 100 KB per second

- GPS: 50 KB per second

- LIDAR: 10 to 70 MB per second

If you add all that up, you get about 4,000 GB per day of data, assuming that a car is being driven about 8 hours per day. As a basis for comparison, it is estimated that the average tech-savvy person uses only about 650 MB per day when you add-up all of the online social media, online video watching, online video chatting, and other such uses on a typical day.

The estimates of the data amounts being collected by self-driving cars varies somewhat by the various analysts and experts that are commenting about the data deluge. For example, it is said that Google Waymo's self-driving cars are generating about 1 GB every second while on the road, which makes it 60 GB per hour, and thus for 8 hours it would be about 480 GB. Based on how much time the average human driver drives a car annually, it would be around 2 petabytes of data per year if you used the Waymo suggested collection rate of data.

There's not much point about arguing how much data per se is being collected, and instead we need to focus on the simple and clear cut fact that it is a lot of data. A barrage of data. A torrent of data. And that's a good thing for this reason – the more data we have, the greater the chances of using it wisely for doing machine learning. Notice that I said we need to use the data wisely. If we just feed all this raw data into just anything that we call "machine learning" the results will not likely be very useful. Keep in mind that machine learning is not magic.

It cannot miraculously turn data into supreme knowledge.

The data being fed into machine learning algorithms needs to be pre-processed in various fashions. The machine learning algorithms need to be setup to train on the datasets and adjust their internal parameters correspondingly to what is found. One of the dangers of most machine learning algorithms is that what they have "learned" becomes a hidden morass of internal mathematical aspects. We cannot dig into this and figure out why it knows what it knows. There is no particular logical explanation for what it deems to be "knowledge" about what it is doing.

This is one of the great divides between more conventional AI programming and the purists approach to machine learning. In conventional AI programming, the human developer has used some form of logic and explicit rules to setup the system. For machine learning, it is typically algorithms that merely mathematically adjust based on data patterns, but you cannot in some sense poke into it to find out "why" it believes something to be the case.

Let's take an example of making a right turn on red. One approach to programing a self-driving car would be to indicate that if it "sees" a red light and if it wants to make a right turn, it can come to a stop at the rightmost lane, verify that there isn't anyone in the pedestrian walkway, verify that there is no oncoming traffic to block the turn, and then can make the right turn. This is all a logical step-by-step approach. We can use the camera on the self-driving car to detect the red light, we can use the radar to detect if there are any pedestrians in the walkway, and we can use the LIDAR to detect if any cars are oncoming. The sensory devices generate their data, and the AI of the self-driving car fuses the data together, applies the rules it has been programmed with, and then makes the right turn accordingly.

Compare this approach to a machine learning approach. We could collect data involving cars that are making right turns at red lights. We feed that into a machine learning algorithm. It might ultimately identify that the red light is associated with the cars coming to a halt. It might ultimately identify that the cars only move forward to do the right turn when there aren't any pedestrians in the walkway, etc. This can be accomplished in a supervised manner, wherein the machine learning is guided toward these aspects, or in an unsupervised manner, meaning that it "discovers" these facets without direct guidance.

Similar to my comments earlier regarding learning about birds, the machine learning approach to learning about right turns on red would need an enormous amount of data to figure out the various complexities of the turn aspects. It might also figure out things that aren't related and yet believe that they are. Suppose that the data had a pattern that a right turn on red typically took place when there was a mailbox at the corner. It might therefore expect to detect a mailbox on a corner and only be willing to make the right turn when one is there, and otherwise refuse to make the right turn on red.

There would be no easy way to inspect the machine learning algorithm to ferret out what it assumed was the case for making the right turn on red. For example, in small-scale artificial neural network we can often inspect the weights and values to try and reverse engineer into what the "logic" might be, but for massive-sized neural networks this is not readily feasible. There are some innovative approaches emerging to try and do this, but by-and-large for large-scale settings it is pretty much a mystery. We cannot explain what it is doing, while in the approach of conventional AI programming we could do so (the rules of the road approach).

In spite of these limitations about machine learning, it has the great advantage that rather than trying to program everything in a conventional AI way, which takes specialized programmers hours and hours to do, and which might not even cover all various potentialities, the machine learning algorithm can pretty much run on its own. The machine learning algorithm can merely consume processing cycles and keep running until it seems to find useful patterns. It might also discover facets that weren't apparent to what the human developers might have known.

This is not to suggest that we must choose between using a machine learning approach versus a more conventional AI programming approach. It is not a one-size-fits all kind of circumstance. Complex systems such as self-driving cars consist of a mixture of both approaches. Some elements are based on machine learning, while other elements are based on conventional AI programming. They work hand-in-hand.

Suppose though that you are developing a self-driving car and you don't have sufficient data to turn loose a machine learning algorithm onto? This is one of the current issues being debated at times loudly in the halls of self-driving car makers and the industry.

If you believe that humanity deserves to have self-driving cars, you might then take the position that whomever has self-driving car data ought to make it available to others. For example, some believe that Tesla should make available its self-driving car data and allow other self-driving car makers to make use of it. Likewise, some believe that Google Waymo should share its self-driving car data. If Tesla and Google were to readily share their data, presumably all the other self-driving car makers could leverage it and be able to more readily make viable self-driving cars.

On the other hand, it seems a bit over-the-top to assert that private companies that have invested heavily into developing self-driving cars and that have amassed data at their own costs should have to suddenly turn it over to their competitors. Why should they provide a competitor with something that will allow the competitor to have avoided similar costs? Why should they be enabling their competitors to easily catch-up with them and not have to make similar investments? You can imagine that the self-driving car makers that have such precious data argue that this data is proprietary and not to be handed-out to whomever wants it.

There are some publicly available datasets of driving data, but they are relatively small and sparse. Some have argued that the government should be collecting and providing driving data, making it available to anyone that wants to have it. There are also more complicated questions too, such as what the data should consist of, and in what way would be it representative. In other words, if you have driving data of only driving on perhaps the roads in Palo Alto, does that provide sufficiently generalizable data that machine learning could achieve an appropriate driving ability in Boston or New York?

Most of this data so far is based on self-driving cars, which makes sense because those are the cars that have all the needed sensory devices to collect the data. Another approach involves taking a human-driven car, put the sensory devices onto it, and use that data to learn from. This certainly makes perhaps even more sense to do, in that why try to learn from a self-driving car which is already just a novice at driving, and instead try to learn from the maneuvers of a human driven car that presumably involves a savvy driver and savvy driving.

This is reminiscent of a famous story that occurred during World War II. When Allied bombers returned to their bases, the planes were studied to determine where the holes were. The thinking was that those holes are vulnerable places on the plane and should be armored heavily on future planes, hoping to ensure that those future planes would be able to sustain the aerial attacks better than the existing planes. A mathematician involved in the analysis had a different idea. He pointed out that the planes that didn't return were the ones that had been shot down. The holes on those planes would be the spots to be armored. This was thinking outside-the-box and makes perfectly good sense when you consider it.

The same can be said of collecting self-driving car data. Right now, we are obsessed with collecting the data from self-driving cars, but it might be more sensible to also collect the data from human driven cars. We could include not only well-driven human-driven cars, but also human drivers that are prone to accidents. In this manner, the machine learning algorithm could try to discern between proper driving and improper driving. The improper driving would help keep the self-driving car from falling into the trap of driving in the same ways that bad drivers drive.

For those that believe fervently that self-driving cars will change society and democratize the world, they are pushing toward trying to make all data about self-driving cars available to all comers. Will regulators agree and force companies to do so? Will companies want to voluntarily provide their data? Should this data be made available but perhaps at a fee that would compensate those companies that provide it? Will the data become a privacy issue if it provides a capability to drill into the data down to the actual driving of a particular car? When there are accidents involving self-driving cars, will this data be available for purposes of lawsuits?

We are just starting to see an awareness about the importance of data when it comes to self-driving cars. Up until now, the innovators trying to move forward on self-driving cars have been doing their own thing. As the self-driving car market matures, we're likely to see increased attention to the data and how and who should have the data. Machine learning algorithms hunger for data. Feeding them is essential to ongoing advances of self-driving cars. Society is going to bring pressures into this field of endeavor and I assure you that the question of whether the self-driving car data is proprietary or shared is going to one day become a highly visible and contentious topic. Right now, it's only known to those in the know. Be on the watch for this to break into the limelight, sooner rather than later.

CHAPTER 4

EDGE PROBLEMS AT CORE OF SELF-DRIVING CARS

CHAPTER 4

EDGE PROBLEMS AT CORE
OF SELF-DRIVING CARS

Whenever there is a final piece to a puzzle that is very hard to solve, it often referred to as achieving the "last mile." This colloquial phrase arose from the telecommunications industry and has been based on the notion that the final leg of reaching a customer is often the most costly and arduous to undertake. We might layout fiber optical cable underground along a neighborhood street, but then the real difficulty comes to extending it to reach each household on that block. Physically connecting to the customer premises becomes a logistically enormous problem and one that is not readily solved under reasonable cost and time constraints.

This same phenomenon is found throughout our daily lives. We can often get something 80% or 90% or even 99% done, and then get stuck at that final 20% or 10% or 1% at the end. Now, sometimes, that last piece is not necessarily overly essential and so whether you can get that final oomph or not might not be crucial. In other cases, the final aspect determines whether the entire effort was successful. Imagine flying troops to a foreign land, they rope down from a helicopter hovering over a bad guys domicile, they break down the door of the property, they rush into the place, but then the evil doer manages to escape out a hidden passageway. After all of that effort, after all that likely preparation, and yet in the "last mile" things went awry and so the entire mission is for not.

The word "mile" in this context is not to be taken literally as a distance indicator. Instead, it is to be considered a metaphor for whatever is the last bit of something that needs to be done. You are at work, you are putting together an important presentation for the head of the company. You slave away for days to put together the presentation. On the day of the presentation, you get dressed-up in your finest work clothes, and you rehearse the presentation over and over. Finally, the meeting time arrives, you go to the conference room to make your presentation. The company head is there, waiting impatiently to see and hear your presentation. You load-up your presentation and connect to the screen. But, it turns out, the screen won't work. You are stuck. You try to wave your hands in the air and pretend that the presentation is being shown, but that "last mile" undermined you. Hope this story didn't give you a nightmare.

Anyway, there is a "last mile" that we are facing in the self-driving cars realm. If not figured out, this last piece of the puzzle will prevent self-driving cars from achieving true self-driving car capabilities. Right now, self-driving cars are not true self-driving cars in the sense that we don't yet have a Level 5 self-driving car. We aren't going to ultimately have Level 5 self-driving cars if we don't solve the "last mile" aspects.

At the Cybernetics Self-Driving Car Institute, we are specifically focusing on the "last mile" of software needed to ultimately arrive at true self-driving cars. We are doing this by concentrating on the "edge problems" that few others are currently thinking about.

What is an "edge problem" you might ask? In computer science, we often carve up a problem into its core and then identify other portions that we claim to be at the edge of the problem. This is a classic divide-and-conquer approach to solving problems. You tackle what you believe to be the most essential aspect of the problem and delay dealing with the other parts. Often, this is done because the so-called edges of the problem are vexing. They are extremely difficult to solve and you don't want to postpone making progress by inadvertently trying to tackle the hardest part of the overall problem.

Indeed, today's self-driving car makers are primarily dealing with what most would perceive as the core of the driving task. This entails having a car be able to drive along a road. You can use relatively straightforward and at times simplistic methods to have a car drive down a road. For a highway, you have the sensors detect the lane markings of the highway. By finding those, you now have identified a lane into which you can have the car drive. There's a striped line the right of the car, and another striped line to the left of the car, both of which provide a kind of virtual rails like for a train into which you just need to keep the car confined. You next use the sensors to detect a car ahead of you. You then have your car follow that car that's ahead, and play a kind of pied piper game. As that car ahead speeds-up, you speed-up. If it slows down, you slow down.

Many novice human drivers such as teenagers who are learning to drive will use this same approach to driving. They watch what other cars do, and even if the teenager doesn't comprehend all the other aspects surrounding the driving task (road signs are overwhelming, watching for pedestrians is distracting, etc.), they can at least do the simplistic follow-the-leader tactic. You've probably noticed that most of the existing self-driving cars act in the same way. You as the human must first navigate the car into a situation that allows for this simplistic approach to be used. For example, you drive your car from your house onto the local freeway, and once you are safely on the freeway, you then engage the self-driving car capability. It is about the same as using cruise control, which we've had for many years. You as the human do the "hard" work of getting the car into a circumstance whereby the myopic piece of AI automation can then perform its task.

The amount of intelligence embodied in today's self-driving cars is quite shallow. Shallow is a way we use to describe whether an AI system is robust or whether it is brittle. A shallow AI system is only able to do a particular task, and once you start to go outside a rather confining scope, the AI system is no longer able to cope with the situation. Today's self-driving cars demand that a human driver be instantly ready to intervene for the AI of the self-driving car, once it gets itself at the bounds of what it can do. These bounds aren't impressive and so the human must be ready at all times to intervene. Only if you have a pristine driving situation is the AI able to proceed without human intervention.

Thus, if you are on a freeway or highway, and if it is a nice sunny day, and if the traffic is clearly apparent around you, and if the surface of the road is normal, and if there aren't any other kinds of nuances or extraordinary aspects, the self-driving car can kind of drive the car. Toss even the slightest exception into the mix, and the self-driving car is going to ask you as the human driver to intervene. This ability of the AI is good enough perhaps for a Level 2 or maybe a Level 3 self-driving car, but we aren't going to get readily to a safe Level 4 and certainly not at all to a true Level 5 if we continue down this path of assuming a straightforward driving environment.

I am not saying that we shouldn't be proud of what self-driving cars are now able to undertake. Pushing forward on self-driving car technology is essential toward making progress, even if done incrementally. As I have stated throughout this book, Google's approach of aiming for the Level 5 self-driving car has been laudable, and while we've seen Tesla aim at the lower levels of self-driving cars, we need someone coming along at the lower levels to gain acceptance for self-driving cars and spur momentum toward the Level 5. Google has concentrated on experiments, while Tesla has concentrated on day-to-day driving. Both approaches are crucial. We need the practical, everyday experience that the Tesla and other existing self-driving cars are providing, but we also need the moonshot approaches such as that of Google (though, as I've mentioned, Google too has now shifted toward the let's-get-something onto today's roads too).

I've been pressing continually about the various edge problems that confront the self-driving car marketplace. These edge problems are the "last mile" that will determine our ability to reach Level 4 and Level 5. Solving these edge problems also aids the Level 2 and Level 3 self-driving cars, but they are in a sense merely considered "handy" for Level 2 and Level 3 (helpful to improving the self-driving car at those levels), while they are a key necessity for Level 4 and Level 5.

Here's a brief indication of the AI software components that we are developing at the Cybernetics Self-Driving Car Institute, of which I'll reveal just those aspects that we have publicly described (there are other additional "stealth" related efforts underway too that I won't be mentioning herein; sorry, can't give out all of our secrets!):

Pedestrian behavior prediction

Today's self-driving cars are crudely able to detect that a pedestrian is standing in the middle of the street, and so the AI core then will try to come to stop or take an avoidance action to keep from running into the pedestrian. But, there is almost no capability today of trying to in-advance predict pedestrian behavior. If a pedestrian is on the sidewalk and running toward the street, this is essentially undetected today (it is not something that the AI system has been programmed to be concerned about). Only once the self-driving car and the pedestrian are in imminent danger of colliding, and in an obvious manner, does the AI core realize that something is amiss. Unfortunately, this lack of in-advance anticipation leads to circumstances whereby there is little viable way to safely deal with the pending accident. Our AI component, in contrast, can help predict that the pedestrian is going to enter into the street and potentially create an accident with dire consequences, and thus provide greater opportunity for the self-driving car to take avoidance actions. By solving this edge problem aspect, it will greatly improve self-driving cars at all levels of the SAE scale, it will reduce the chances of accidents involving pedestrians, and will be needed definitely to achieve the true Level 5. Besides predicting pedestrian behavior, we are also including the predictive behavior of actions by bicyclists and motorcyclists.

Roundabouts

It's admittedly not every day that you encounter a roundabout, also known as a traffic circle or a rotary. But, when you do encounter it, you need to know how to navigate it. Self-driving cars treat this as an edge problem, something that they aren't worried about right now as it is an exception rather than a common driving situation. We are developing AI software to plug into a self-driving car's core AI and provide a capability to properly and safely traverse a roundabout.

Conspicuity

When humans are driving a car, they use the car in conspicuous ways to try and warn other drivers and pedestrians. This includes using the headlights, the horn, various special maneuvers, etc. Self-driving car makers aren't yet incorporating these acts of conspicuousness into their AI, since it is not considered core to today's driving tasks. But, in order to achieve Level 4 and Level 5, these are edge problem aspects will be a differentiator for self-driving car makers.

Accident scene traversal

When a self-driving car today happens to come upon an accident scene, the AI hands over the driving of the car to the human driver since its core doesn't know what to do. This is because an accident scene has numerous driving exceptions that the AI is not yet able to cope with, it's an edge problem. Our software allows for the AI to invoke specialized routines that know what accident scene consists of and how to have the self-driving car can safely make its way through or around it.

Emergency vehicle awareness

As humans, we are aware that we need to be listening for sirens that indicate an emergency vehicle is near our car and we then need to pull over and let the emergency vehicle proceed. Or, maybe we see the flashing lights of the emergency vehicle and must make decisions about whether to speed-up or slow down, or take other evasive actions with our cars. This is not considered a core problem by the existing AI systems for self-driving cars, instead it's considered an exception or edge problem. We are developing AI software that provides this specialized capability.

Left turns advanced-capabilities

The left turn is notorious for being considered a dangerous act when driving a car. Though self-driving cars have a traditional left-turn capability at their core, whenever a particular thorny or difficult left-turn arises the self-driving car tends to hand the controls back to the human driver. These are considered edge problem left-turns. This is a risky gambit though to hand things over to the human, as the human driver is thrust into a dicey left-turn situation at the last moment, plus, this handing over of control to a human is not allowed at Level 5. We are developing AI software that handles these worst case scenario left-turns.

Self-driving in midst of human driven cars

Most of the self-driving cars today assume that other cars will be driven by humans that are willing to play nicely with the self-driving car. If a human decides to suddenly swerve toward the self-driving car, the simplistic core aspects don't know what to do, other than make pre-programmed radical maneuvers or hand the controls over to the human driver. We are developing AI software that comprehends the ways that human drivers drive and assumes that a true self-driving car has to know how to contend with human driving foibles.

Roadway debris reactions

Self-driving cars are able to use their sensors to detect roadway debris, but the AI core right now tends to not know what to do once the debris is detected. Deciding whether to try and roll over the debris or swerve to avoid it, this is considered currently an edge problem. Usually, the self-driving car just hands control to the human driver, but this can be a troubling moment for the human driver to react to, and also there isn't going to be a human driver available in Level 5. We are developing AI software that aids in detecting debris and providing self-driving car tactics to best deal with the debris.

Road sign interpretation

Self-driving cars are often not scanning for and interpreting road signs. They tend to rely upon their GPS to figure out aspects such as speed limits and the like, rather than searching for and interpreting road signs. This though is a crucial edge problem in that there are road signs that we encounter that are paramount to the driving task and cannot be found anywhere else other than as the car drives past the road sign. For example, when roadwork is being done and temporary road signs have been placed out to warn about the driving conditions. We are developing AI software that does this road sign detection and interpretation.

Human behavior assessment

Today's self-driving cars do not have at their AI core the ability to look at other humans and detect their motions and indications about the driving task. For example, suppose you come up to an intersection that the lights are out, and so a traffic officer is directing traffic. This is considered an edge problem by today's AI developers. If you are in a self-driving car and it encounters this situation, and even if it can figure out what is going on, it will just hand over control of driving to you. This can be dangerous as a hand-off issue, and also it is not allowed for a Level 5. We are developing software that can detect and interpret the actions of humans that are part of the ecosystem of the self-driving car.

As mentioned, these kinds of edge problems are seen by many of the existing car makers as not currently crucial to the AI core of the self-driving task. This makes sense if you are merely wanting to get a self-driving car to drive along a normal road in normal conditions, and if you assume that you will always have an attentive human driver ready to be handed the controls of the car. These baby steps of limited scope for the AI core toward a self-driving car are going to though backfire when we get more self-driving cars on the roadways, and the human drivers in those self-driving cars become less attentive and less aware of what is expected of them in the mix between the AI driving the car and their driving of the car.

Furthermore, solving these "edge problems" is essential if we are to achieve Level 5. By the way, these edge problems involve driving situations that we encounter every day, and are not some farfetched aspects. Sometimes, an edge problem in computer science is a circumstance that only happens once in a blue moon. Those kinds of infrequent edge problems can at times be delayed in solving, since we assume that there's a one in a million chance of ever encountering that particular problem.

For the edge problems I've identified here, any of these above driving situations can occur at any time, on any roadway, in any locale, and under normal driving conditions. These are not unusual or rare circumstances. They involve driving tasks that we take for granted. Novice drivers are at first not familiar with these situations and so over time tend to learn how to cope with them. We are using AI techniques along with machine learning to push self-driving cars up the learning curve and be able to properly handle these edge problems.

We are also exploring the more extraordinary circumstances, involving extraordinary driving conditions that only happen rarely, but first it makes most sense to focus on the everyday driving that we would want self-driving cars to be able to handle, regardless of their SAE level of proficiency. Some of the development team liken this notion to the ways in which we've seen Operating Systems evolve over time. A core Operating System such as Microsoft Windows at first didn't provide a capability to detect and deal with computer viruses, and so there were separate components that arose for that purpose. Gradually, those computer anti-virus capabilities were eventually incorporated into the core part of the Operating System.

We envision that our AI edge problem components will likewise be at first add-ons to the core of the AI self-driving car, and then, over time, the core will come to integrate these capabilities directly into the AI mainstay for the self-driving cars. We'll meanwhile be a step ahead, continually pushing at the boundaries and providing added new features that will improve self-driving car AI capabilities.

Sometimes, edge problems are also referred to as "wicked problems" and this is due to the aspect that they are very hard to solve and seemingly intractable. These are exactly the kinds of problems we enjoy solving at the Cybernetic Self-Driving Car Institute. By solving wicked problems, aka edge problems, we can ensure that self-driving cars are safer, more adept at the driving task, and will ultimately reach the vaunted true Level 5. We encourage you to do likewise and help us all solve these thorny edge problems of the self-driving car task. Drive safely out there.

.

CHAPTER 5

SOLVING THE ROUNDABOUT TRAVERSAL PROBLEM FOR SELF-DRIVING CARS

CHAPTER 5

SOLVING THE ROUNDABOUT TRAVERAL PROBLEM FOR SELF-DRIVING CARS

Help, I am stuck in a roundabout and can't get out.

For those of you that have ever driven into a roundabout, often also known as a traffic circle, a road circle, and sometimes a rotary, they can be devilish to navigate. Typically, a novice driver finds them to be frightening and a real-world version of a crazy bumper car mad dash. Seasoned drivers like to think that they have mastered the roundabout and so act like it is a breeze to traverse one. Even the seasoned drivers though are at times thrown for a loop and find themselves baffled and tortured by the roundabout. If you get enough drivers going through a roundabout and if they are all behaving badly, you find yourself wishing you had gone some other path and had avoided the dreaded roundabout.

As the head of the Cybernetics Self-Driving Car Institute, we've been developing techniques and software to enable self-driving cars to properly traverse a roundabout.

Most of today's self-driving cars hand the driving back to the human driver when encountering a roundabout. That's if the self-driving car even realizes that a roundabout is about to occur or occurring. Some self-driving cars head into a roundabout without the realization that it is a roundabout. The AI of the self-driving car is often ill-prepared for the specific dynamics of a roundabout. As such, the AI either struggles to make it through the traffic circle safely, or at the last moment is gives up and tosses control of the vehicle to the human driver. This is not only dangerous for the human driver and passengers, since the act of taking over control suddenly can be disruptive and create confusion for the human driver, it also violates the principle of the Level 5 true self-driving car which is that the AI must be able to do whatever driving a human driver could do. In that sense, we need to have a solution for roundabouts if we are going to achieve Level 5 self-driving cars, which we are still some distance from achieving.

For those of you that have rarely if ever encountered a roundabout, they aren't especially common in the United States, numbering an estimated 3,000 or so across the entire country. In contrast, if you've ever been to Europe, and especially France, you'd have seen quite a number of these roundabouts. France has the fame of having the most roundabouts in the world, numbering around 30,000, so about ten times the number of roundabouts in the entire United States. Given the size of France in comparison to the United States, the per capita or per square mile ratio of the number of roundabouts is extremely high in France.

The United States has had roundabouts since before the advent of the car. Some consider the most famous and early notable roundabout to be the Columbus Circle in New York City (shout out to NYC!), which was designed and put into place around 1905. There are numerous studies about roundabouts and all sorts of engineering aspects underlying them. Traffic engineers tend to like the roundabout. It is a means to regulate traffic flow. In theory, it is as safe if not safer than a conventional intersection, it flows traffic more smoothly, it reduces wasted fuel consumption in comparison to having cars sit at a traffic light of a conventional intersection, it produces less pollutants because again the cars aren't sitting at an intersection, and otherwise it is just kind of cool. The Traffic Research Laboratory (TRL) provides very helpful analyses of roundabouts, particularly the ones in the United States, and provides a somewhat definitive guide to the topic.

There are a myriad of variants of a roundabout. There are mini-roundabouts, magical roundabouts, there are roundabouts in city settings, ones in suburban settings, ones nearby to schools, etc. I won't cover all the variants here, and focus instead on the overall model of a roundabout. If a self-driving car can handle a modestly complex generic roundabout, it can then tailor to whatever specific circumstance it faces for a particular roundabout. But, if the AI lacks any knowledge of a roundabout, its overall driving rules and capabilities are likely going to get it into trouble and so the need for a specialized component to guide it during the roundabout traversal.

You might wonder why traffic engineers believe that a roundabout is safer than conventional intersections. When you have wandered into a roundabout with lots of other traffic, it often seems to be like a swirling pit of man-eating sharks, and you might think it has to be the least safe way to ever design any kind of traffic flow. According to the stats collected by the TRL, they claim that it is actually much safer than conventional intersections. Part of the logic is that when you come to a conventional intersection, you have the chance of ramming other cars at right-angles, you have a chance at hitting other cars at a heads-on position, and you have a chance at hitting other cars during a left turn. All of those aspects are generally eliminated via the roundabout. For the roundabout, you mainly have the chances of doing glancing blows off of other vehicles. Rarely do those glancing blows then lead into a full-fledged derby style cascade of cars knocking into each other. Of course, you also have the risk of rear ending other cars, such as when you first try to enter into the traffic circle, and when you try to exit the traffic circle. These roundabouts are certainly not risk free, even if in theory "safer" than conventional intersections.

What constitutes a roundabout? The usual roundabout is composed of an inner core that is an island, upon which no cars are allowed to go. Traffic flowing to the roundabout usually comes from 360 degrees around the island. The lanes flowing into the circular area are at staggered positions around the circle. Roundabouts typically will have two to four such entrances into the circular flow. There are usually concentric circular lanes surrounding the roundabout. Sometimes there is only one such lane, into which the entering traffic must squeeze. More often, there are two or more circular lanes, referred to as multi-lane roundabouts. Traffic flowing around the circle jockeys into and out of these concentric circular lanes. There are inner lanes that are closest to the island, and outer lanes.

You have to somehow enter into the roundabout, and somehow exit from the roundabout. The entrance lanes are usually posted with a Yield sign and the driver must yield to the traffic already flowing around the circle. In addition to entrance lanes, there are exit lanes. The exit lanes will sometimes be separated from the entrance lanes and are their own distinct lanes. More often, the entrance and exit lanes are aligned with each other, but usually there is a separator to try and ensure that exiting traffic doesn't inadvertently try to go into an entrance lane. Between the entrance lane and an exit lane there are often splitters that keep those separated from each other. A splitter is an area marked for cars not to go onto it, which can be an actual raised median or it can be just painted onto the ground.

The core island of the roundabout is sometimes just a painted marked area, but more often it is a raised island and has something on it. It might be covered with grass or other low-to-ground aspects, allowing the drivers to see across the island and be able to detect traffic that is on the other side of the roundabout. Most cities though try to make the island into something noticeable and attractive, and so they put artwork there, such as statue of the founding figures of the city, or they put a fountain that is spitting out water and provides a nice respite from the visual dullness of cars flowing around and around of the roundabout.

For self-driving cars, this aspect that the island has something on it can be an added difficulty factor when trying to traverse the roundabout. The sensors of the self-driving car are not readily able to penetrate whatever is on the island, and so it limits an ability to predict traffic patterns. The cameras of the self-driving car and the LIDAR and radar are only able to get a partial indication of what traffic is on the other side of the island, and not able to gain a full sense of the other cars that are then coming ultimately toward the self-driving car via the concentric circles. It is still worthwhile to try and get that data in real-time and analyze it, but the AI of the self-driving car has to assume that the data will be noisy, obscured, and only provide at best partial information about what is taking place on the other side of the island.

Let's now take a look at how the self-driving car can properly traverse a roundabout.

First, the AI should be doing a look-ahead to anticipate a roundabout. Via GPS, the AI can potentially already be aware that a roundabout is part of the route being traveled. If so, the AI might determine that trying to deal with the roundabout is not worth the trouble and instead opt to find an alternative route via the GPS that eliminates the need to traverse the roundabout. Assuming that the alternatives do not otherwise significantly raise the time required for travel or have other adverse consequences, it is often feasible to simply skirt around a roundabout and take some other viable path.

Suppose there is no other viable path, or suppose that the GPS is either not available or has failed to realize that a roundabout is soon to be encountered, the AI needs to be ready to handle the roundabout. Often, there are street signs that indicate a roundabout is upcoming. The AI might be forewarned that a roundabout is imminent as a result of reading a street sign, and so either opt to avoid the roundabout at the last minute and find an alternative path, or at least begin to prepare for the advent of the roundabout.

Upon arriving at an entrance to the roundabout, the AI needs to use its sensors to ascertain how many lanes are combined into this particular entrance. If there is only one lane, then the self-driving car has a simplified task since it only needs to focus on getting into the circular traffic that is flowing around the roundabout. Things become more complex when there are two or more lanes that combine into the particular entrance that the self-driving car is using. In such a case, the AI needs to now observe the cars that are in the aligned lanes of the entrance. These cars can be a mixture of human driven cars and self-driving cars, either of which will be potentially hard to predict in terms of driving behavior.

The next aspects of traversal can be potentially guided by machine learning, if the self-driving car has prior data associated with this roundabout, and if the prior data has been analyzed by the machine learning to identify patterns for best navigating the roundabout. This could be the case if there are many self-driving cars that have been using the roundabout and then feeding their data into a global data collection for use by the machine learning. For now, we'll assume this is unlikely to be available and that the AI will need to directly try to mentally muscle its way through the roundabout.

When two or more lanes exist in one entrance, the cars at the front of the line that are seeking to enter into the circular flow of traffic will tend to jockey to see which makes the first move into traffic. Furthermore, if say another car is immediately to the left of the self-driving car, and if that car decides to dart into traffic, it potentially cuts off the self-driving car from being able to make its move into traffic.

The AI needs to detect the cars aligned in the entrance and ascertain the nature of their behavior as to whether aggressively inching forward or being at a halt.

This brings up another aspect namely that if the conditions are proper, the self-driving car can directly feed into the circular flow of traffic, without having to come to halt or even potentially slow down. As the self-driving car makes its way into the entrance, the normal driving control would be to slow down so as to allow for judging of making a move into the circular flow of traffic. In fact, roundabouts are known for their "traffic calming" effect in that the cars coming to the entrances will usually decrease speeds in order to obey a yield to the flowing traffic.

There are though sometimes "perfect conditions" in which the self-driving car can smoothly come to the entrance and then continue unabated into the circular flow. For example, if there is no other traffic already on the circular flow, or if the traffic in the circular flow has provided an appropriate gap, the self-driving car can make one continues shift from the entrance and into the outer lane of the circular flow.

One of the most arduous analyses for the roundabout indeed involves finding a gap in the circular flow that will safely allow the self-driving car to makes its way into the circular flow. Humans often have a tendency to make a gap, called gap-acceptance, allowing an entering car to gain entry into the circular flow. Some drivers while driving the circular flow will purposely slow down or speed-up in anticipation of allowing a car to move from the entrance into the flow. Of course, there are other drivers that either don't care about providing a gap, or even take the opposite stance and intentionally cut-off the entrant from entering into the flow. This varies depending upon the time of day, the day of the week, the volume and velocity of traffic, and the local cultural norms concerning the particular roundabout.

Once into the circular flow, the self-driving car usually starts at the outer lane of the concentric circles, assuming there is more than one such lane. Part of the analysis now becomes whether the AI should guide the self-driving car toward the inner lane of the circular flow or remain in an outer lane. If the exit for the self-driving car is quickly approaching, the AI should keep the self-driving car in the outer lane. If the exit is on the other side of the circle, making movement into the inner lane can be beneficial, and avoid the rather chaotic aspects that occur on the outer lane. The outer lane is a continual frenzy of cars gaining entrance and exiting, and there is at times a greater calm to be found by moving into the inner lane.

As the self-driving car nears the desired exit, it needs to make its way to the outer lane, assuming it is not already there. If other cars are unwilling to allow the self-driving car to jockey out to the outer lane, it is conceivable that one full iteration of the circle might be needed to accommodate getting over to the needed outer lane. Observations of human drivers shows that they will often take this same tact. Namely, they have become trapped in the inner lane and the surrounding traffic won't let them safely make their way to the outer lane. This can be the fault of the human driver for not having started toward the outer lane soon enough to make it to the desired exit. The self-driving car should be able to appropriately ascertain the distances and the lanes to early enough start to make a move toward the outer lane and ultimately be in a position to make the exit.

But, this transition from the inner lane to the outer lane is contingent on the behavior of the other drivers. If the other drivers are stubbornly not allowing the inner lane self-driving car to make its way to the outer lane, it might be necessary to make a full revolution and therefore seek a more favorable condition on the next round. Presumably, the cars that were purposely blocking the move will by now have exited themselves from the circular flow of traffic, and hopefully other remaining cars will allow for a movement out of the inner lane.

The behavioral aspects of drivers in roundabouts is a crucial element in traversing the roundabout. Legally, most roundabouts are designated such that the cars entering into the circle must yield to those cars already flowing in the circle. What happens in actual practice can differ significantly. In fact, "priority reversal" occurs quite often, whereby the cars entering into the circle don't wait their turn, and instead they force themselves into the circle. This causes cars that are already in the circular flow to have to yield to those brash entrants. This can become a dangerous game, since the entrants are nearly daring the already flowing cars to hit them, and in this game of chicken somebody has to give way.

In terms of the exit from the roundabout, the self-driving car needs to make its way to the outer lane and then flow into the desired exit. This can be made more arduous by other cars that are trying to get past the exiting car and at times block the exit for the exiting car. Once again, if needed, the self-driving car might need to abandon its attempt to achieve the exit and make another loop around the roundabout. The nature of the allowed aggressiveness of the self-driving car will partially determine whether it can quickly make the loop and exit, or whether it will need to possibly make multiple loops.

Most of the self-driving cars today are programmed to be the "old granny" style driver. The AI takes an ultra-conservative approach to driving the car. Furthermore, any more aggressive actions are simply handed over to the human driver, rather than having the self-driving car take such actions. This timid style is sensible during the existing era of trying to get self-driving cars to be simplistic drivers on the roads, but eventually we'll need to ratchet up the aggressiveness of self-driving cars.

After the self-driving car has made its way to the desired exit, there is usually a need to speed-up at that point. The exits from most roundabouts tend to flow back into normal street traffic, and so the self-driving car needs to accelerate from what was likely a slower speed during the roundabout and into a faster speed to match with the traffic flow beyond the exit. It is also conceivable that the self-driving car might have gotten itself mired in the roundabout and taken an exit by mistake, which, if so, the self-driving car would now need to recalculate how to get back onto whatever path was supposed to be taken. We are all used to this when we hear our GPS say "recalculating" after we've taken the wrong turn. I know that it seems unimaginable to think that the self-driving car would have taken the wrong exit, since we expect that a self-driving car is to be perfect, but, if the roundabout has become high risk it might make better sense to get out of it, rather than pursuing "perfection" for the desired exit and yet put the occupants at undue risk to do so.

In spite of the overall notion that roundabouts are safer than conventional intersections, there are certainly many ways in which a self-driving car can get itself into hot water in a roundabout. Upon entering into the roundabout, the self-driving car could inadvertently rear-end another car that has tried to cut-off the self-driving car or that was in the loop and suddenly decide to brake. Once inside the flow of the roundabout, other cars trying to weave into and out of the concentric lanes can readily strike the self-driving car. Cars coming into the roundabout that are behind a self-driving car might become impatient and rear-end the self-driving car. And, as mentioned earlier, there are lots of chances for having glancing blows among cars that are in the concentric circles.

Besides developing AI software for dealing with the particulars of roundabouts, we are also doing simulations to gauge how well the AI can deal with the uncertainties associated with roundabouts. We purposely feed "human driven" cars into the roundabout that consist of humans that are the Indy race car driver type that thinks the roundabout is fun and intended for battle, and we feed into it the timid drivers that drive into a roundabout once a year or once in a lifetime and mess-up the flow by going slowly and not abiding by the flow of traffic. These real-world simulations help the AI to learn how to deal with the variety of human drivers that will be encountered while traversing a roundabout.

.

CHAPTER 6

PARALLEL PARKING MINDLESS FOR SELF-DRIVING CARS: STEP IT UP

CHAPTER 6

PARALLEL PARKING MINDLESS FOR SELF-DRIVING CARS: STEP IT UP

Most of us have at one time or another tried to parallel park our car and suffered the frustration and at times humiliation that we just could not seem to get the car into that desired space. Back and forth, trying over and over, meanwhile sometimes there is someone watching as we do so, such as pedestrians on the sidewalk or maybe a driver sitting behind you that is waiting for you to get out of their way and just finish that darned parallel parking job. It can be nail biting. Plus, though you aren't willing to likely admit it, I am betting that you probably touched or bumped a car or two while trying to squeeze into a tight parallel parking space. You undoubtedly looked around to see if anyone spotted you doing so, and if not, quickly disembarked from your now parked car and pretended that you had not played bumper cars with strangers.

When you start out as a novice driver, the act of parallel parking seems incredibly difficult. Many teenage drivers that are careful about their driving will purposely avoid doing parallel parking. Those that don't care about other cars are often eager to do parallel parking, tending to do so at a speed and manner that would make their parents become queasy if they knew that their teen driver was muscling their car this way. Elderly are prone to avoid doing parallel parking, partially due to the complexity, but also at times due to the twisting and contortions that as a driver you often need to do, looking backward and over your shoulder as you execute the maneuver. This can make anyone's back and neck be sore, no matter what your age.

Does all of this indicate that parallel parking is a highly complex task? No. In fact, it is a relatively straightforward task. At least when considering the act of carrying out the formulaic parts of the parallel parking task. In a moment, we'll walk through the tasks. As will be shown, this is pretty much a mindless kind of driving task. From an AI perspective, there's not much involved. One might be cynical and say that you could train a monkey to parallel park. By this, I mean that the steps are routine, easily trained, repeatable, and requires almost no human judgment per se.

At the Cybernetics Self-Driving Car Institute, we are aiming at stepping up the parallel parking task in ways that do require human judgment and provide AI specialized software that goes far beyond today's mindless AI used for parallel parking. If you enlarge your viewpoint of the scope of the parallel parking task, you'll see that there are aspects today that are being omitted entirely by self-driving cars that have a so-called parallel parking capability, often called Auto Park or Active Park Assist.

First, what are the steps required to parallel park a car? We'll make our scope narrow and then enlarge it after we've covered the basics of this all-to-common driving task.

Here's what you are normally urged to do:

- Pull alongside the lead parked car, allowing a 3-foot gap parallel between you and it
- Align your back tires with the lead parked car's rear bumper, halt
- Go into reverse and before starting motion turn your wheels hard-right
- Start into motion, backing up slowly, until you are at an angle of 45 degrees, halt
- Now, while not in motion, turn your wheels hard-left
- Continue slowly to back-up, until you are in the spot and parallel with the curb
- If needed, move backward or forward to even out the space ahead and behind you

There are other ways to do parallel parking, but the above is well representative of the recommended approaches. If you've not ever had someone lay out the step-by-step approach, well, guess what, you now know formally how to do parallel parking. Many people were never schooled in how to do so. They learned by trial-and-error. Indeed, some never figured it out and so just chock up the whole thing to a magical method that they can't seem to divine.

The truth be told, there is no magic involved. In the self-driving car industry, you find some that smirk at consumers that marvel at a car that is able to parallel park by itself. What magic! What a wondrous sight to see! The human driver takes their hands off the wheel, and with seemingly a robotic ghost driving the car, it smoothly works its way into a parallel parking space. This must be AI at its finest. Maybe this is a sign that we are soon on the verge of AI taking over the world. We are soon to be slaves of the AI systems that will rule us.

It's a simple parlor trick. Just like watching a magician that makes a coin disappear and magically reappear, once you know the secret of the trick, you realize that there's not much to it.

In this case, the self-driving car uses it sensors to detect that the car is in the right placement to start the parallel parking task. It can use the camera, LIDAR or radar to measure the distance and identify the parked cars that are nearby. It is connected to the car's controls such that it can accelerate and brake as needed, along with being able to turn the steering wheel. Following the above formulaic steps, it carries out those steps. One step, then another. Programmed easily. Indeed, it can do this in an exacting manner and without any emotion, which kind of helps. Human drivers sometimes doubt the approach and misbelieve that they are about to hit the parked car, when in fact there are inches to spare. The radar, camera, and LIDAR are not emotional about this and can make relatively accurate measurements and proceed in a coldly calculated manner.

Human drivers are rushed by another car that has come upon them and are waiting anxiously for you to get out of their way. Or, with pedestrians watching you, you are fearful they are going to record your actions and post it onto YouTube, wherein a million hits will arise of you fumbling to make that parallel parking job. Maybe you reverse too fast, or maybe you don't turn the car wheel far enough. There are lots of ways that a sloppy or nervous human can mess up this procedure. Automation doesn't get distracted by those aspects and in a rote manner carries out what it was programmed to do.

The ability to parallel park is gradually becoming a standard feature on most cars. The automation for it is easy to put into place, once you have the sensors on the car and the automation connected to the controls of the car. The software to do the parallel parking task is easy. It's having the sensors and the controls to drive the car that are "harder" merely because of the cost of the hardware and its needing to be integrated into the car.

In fact, we now have car makers that are crowing about how their parallel parking feature is faster than someone else's. One car maker says their car can parallel park in 1 minute. Another one says it can be done in 30 seconds. Now, we are inching our way down, and the latest benchmark seems to be 24 seconds. This is though really kind of not interesting from an AI viewpoint. Shaving a few seconds off of parallel parking is merely more of the same parlor trick. You can control how fast the car reverses and tweak the formulaic approach, but it is still the same mindless task.

Consumers were surveyed and asked whether they trust their car to do parallel parking (assuming that such a feature is available on their car). Interestingly, only about 25% said they would trust a car to parallel park. If the task is as routine as I claim, why aren't more consumers convinced of the trustworthiness of the parallel parking capability of modern cars?

It could be that consumers are unsure of the formulaic aspects and believe that the task is complex, thus, they assume that the mental abilities of the automation must be quite high to be able to do the task. This makes sense since humans themselves find the task to be bedeviling, and so this carries over into their assumptions about what the automation has to do. Or, it could be that they have rarely seen or used the feature, and so the unknown aspects of whether it really works or not is causing consumers to be hesitant to believe that it works. Maybe after seeing the task done over and over by self-driving cars, humans will eventually believe that it is doable by the automation.

Another explanation has to do with the scope of the parallel parking automation. And, this goes toward my point earlier about how the scope is so constrained that we have taken the judgement out of the equation. Remember that I said earlier that this task is repeatable, simplistic, formulaic, and requires no judgment. Let's enlarge the scope and see if those assumptions continue to hold true.

First, what happens when you initially even conceive of the idea that you might want to parallel park your car? You have reached a juncture where you want to park your car, and presumably there are no other viable choices other than doing a parallel parking action. In other words, you would have looked around, wherever you are, and determine that the only available parking spot, or at least the only most desirable spot, will require you to invoke parallel parking.

There aren't any self-driving cars today that scan the surrounding area to try and detect where you can park your car, and then if identifying that the only viable parking spot requires parallel parking, opt to go into a parallel parking mode. Instead, you, the human driver of the car, need to first find such a spot. Furthermore, you, the human driver, need to drive the car to the spot and position the car into kind of just the right posture for it to then become engaged to do the parallel parking.

This is like having a child that can do only one thing and it is up to you as an adult to guide the child to the precise place that allows the child to perform their one magic trick. Unfortunately, this is not going to be sufficient for Level 5 self-driving cars, in the sense that a Level 5 is supposed to be able to do anything a human driver could do, and so requiring a human occupant to have to identify and then position the self-driving car is not going to work. We'll need the AI to do this.

Next, even if the car is positioned in the right place, today's parallel parking approaches do not take a look at see if the spot is a legally allowed parking space. Suppose there is a sufficient gap to park your car, but the curb is painted red. Today's self-driving cars don't realize this. What about a white painted curb, or a blue painted curb, or yellow, or green? We would want the AI to figure out whether this is a legal spot to park in. This also includes looking at the road signs. There might be a road sign that says no parking in that spot between the hours of 9 a.m. and 5 p.m., and if it is currently noon then you might be inviting yourself into getting a parking ticket. Perhaps there's a fire hydrant there and so you can't park there. Etc.

Alright, let's consider the next aspect, namely, suppose that the spot is blocking a driveway or the sidewalk. This is often a legal issue. Plus, even if in some cases legally allowed, there are some places that parking just doesn't make sense because of the ire of others that park nearby. I've seen angry neighbors that had their driveway partially blocked on a busy July 4th weekend that then decided to run a straight edge along the pretty paint job on the outside of the car. I am not advocating taking the law into your hands, and just emphasizing that there are some spots that might seem viable due to the size of the spot, but there are lots of other considerations that need to be taken into account too.

Identifying the spot to park the car is usually done by simply measuring the gap between the two already parked cars (or, whatever else is serving as the bookends). A typical parallel parking automation will gladly try to fit into a sufficient sized spot, but suppose that someone has parked their bicycle in that same spot. Most of the existing systems don't look for objects that might be in the spot already. There could be a person standing in the spot and trying to reserve it for their friend. Or suppose a child is standing in the spot and looking for their penny that they dropped onto the street near the curb. These obstructions are rarely looked for, and often if scanned for are only found once the self-driving car is already partially into the self-parking operation.

The only criteria being used currently by the automation involves adhering strictly to the formulaic steps, and then aiming to park as close to the curb as feasible, often ending up at a mere half inch away from the curb, and that the automation wants to keep to a minimum the number of maneuvers taken and the number of curb strikes encountered. This criteria is though not very human-like in many respects.

For example, parking a car within a half inch of the curb can be a bad thing to do. When you open the car door, it might brush against the curb. Or, the car door might swing open and hit a standing object on the sidewalk that is adjacent to the parking spot. Humans usually leave about 8 inches, partially by being lousy at parallel parking but also at times because it is more convenient when getting out of and into the car (and there are laws about how far away from the curb you can legally park, plus, how you turn the wheel depending upon whether you are parked on an incline). There are other instances where you purposely do park close to the curb, such as to avoid stepping into a puddle at the curb. These are aspects that a human driver would consider, and for which we should expect any robust AI to also consider.

Let's revisit the earlier point about the aspect that surveys of consumers seem to indicate that they don't trust a self-driving car to do parallel parking. This makes a lot of sense in that the existing parallel parking is being done essentially by a child. The automation is working in a routinized fashion and has no real smarts to it. Why would you trust this? Also, you, the human, need to do so much upfront work to get the car to the proper spot and make sure that it is clear and legal, you might as well finish the job yourself.

I've seen some car owners that show off the parallel parking automation to their friends, and then they opt to never use it again. It is one of those boastful features, but not a truly practical day-to-day feature. Of course, the proud car maker can brag about the feature and advertise it. This works to attract buyers of the car. Once the car is bought, the owner though realizes that it is another one of those fancy features that does not cut the mustard. There it then resides, unused. All because it is insufficient. At the Cybernetics Self-Driving Car Institute, we are developing an advanced parallel parking AI component that will make parallel parking into a smart capability and one that consumers will have faith that it can do the job. Drive safely out there.

CHAPTER 7

CAVEATS OF OPEN SOURCE FOR SELF-DRIVING CARS

Lance B. Eliot

CHAPTER 7

CAVEATS OF OPEN SOURCE FOR SELF-DRIVING CARS

Suppose that someone gave away their software for free.

Are they crazy? Not really. We all know about software "freemium" models nowadays, whereby a software application is made available for free and the trick to monetizing the giveaway involves either posting ads and making money from advertisers, or making money by having the user be willing to purchase add-ons, such as buying additional elements or even lives in an online video game. But suppose they are giving away the actual source code of the software. This is the stuff that is used to actually produce the software application. With the source code, you can essentially make your own software application and do so without much added effort.

Is giving away the source code to software crazy? Some believe it is. Why would someone give away their source code? Believe it or not, in many cases it is done because the software producer is altruistic and genuinely thinks that software should be freely available to all. There are some proponents of open sourcing of software that earnestly have the view that all of mankind would be better off if all software source code was openly available. These do-gooders have a viewpoint about the world that can be difficult for those that are more capitalistic to readily fathom, and often rally around a moral philosophy or a political agenda as the core rationale for open sourcing software.

There are other more economic motivations for open source software too. One perspective is to make available source code to kickstart a marketplace, and then become an expert in that marketplace that can charge for providing advice about the software or by making add-ons to it. This is akin to the freemium model. Yet another approach is sometimes done by academics that want to provide a springboard for research and make advancements in some area of software development. Unbeknownst to those outside the inner realm of the computer aficionados, open source has been a significant niche since nearly the start of the computer era, including the popular operating system known as Linux and the popular web server known as Apache. Google has particularly made open source a known aspect to the masses via their Android operating system, and Microsoft has been brought toward open source, albeit kicking-and-screaming due to the outcries and demands of the marketplace.

What does it truly mean to declare that source code is indeed open source? There is a lot of variability on the matter and some "open source" is actually not very open sourced, meaning that the maker might claim it is open source but they then put tons of restrictions on the licensing aspects of the source code. This is a bit of trick to pretend you have something that is considered open source when in fact it is not. More official definitions of open source say that to be true open source the maker must abide by particular distribution requirements.

The Open Source Initiative (OSI) has a relatively "standardized" definition of open source that commonly is accepted and consists of ten requirements:

1. Free Redistribution – no royalty or other fees, no restriction on selling or giving away the software
2. Source Code – source code must be included and cannot be obfuscated
3. Derived Works – must allow for modifications and derived works, must abide by free original terms
4. Integrity of The Author's Source Code – must not hide who the source code originally came from
5. No Discrimination Against Persons or Groups – cannot restrict certain persons from use
6. No Discrimination Against Fields of Endeavor – cannot

restrict from being used commercially
7. Distribution of License – cannot require added licensing and nor require a non-disclosure agreement
8. License Must Not Be Specific to a Product – cannot embed it into something else that does have restrictions, the original openness must be maintained
9. License Must Not Restrict Other Software – cannot force non-open source to become open source simply due to including this open source
10. License Must Be Technology-Neutral – cannot make the license dependent on a specific technology

This background about open source takes us to the juncture of being able to discuss open source for self-driving cars. There are currently only a handful of bona fide efforts to push toward open source for self-driving cars. These fledgling efforts each have their own motivation. Though it might be nice to think that we are potentially going to produce a full open source model for self-driving cars, I would say it is quite unlikely. As will be explained next, there are lots of reasons that it just isn't going to happen.

Allow me a moment to emphasize that I don't want to crush anybody's dreams, but as you will see there is not going to be sufficient momentum and commitment to produce a fully viable open source self-driving car. Ouch! I know that my assertion hurts for those that are putting their soul into trying to get an open source effort off-the-ground, so to speak, and really my heart does go out to you all. In short, sadly, the odds are not in your favor.

Let's take a look at the three most prominent open source self-driving car attempts: (1) Openpilot, (2) Udacity, and (3) Autoware.

Openpilot has the most chances for some commercial success, but I am anticipating it is going to ultimately peter out and other than offshoots it is not going to be producing a true open source self-driving car. Udacity is an interesting exercise in trying to crowdsource a self-driving car and it will provide a great learning opportunity for many future self-driving car engineers, but it is not going to get us to a true open source self-driving car. Autoware is a handy academic approach and will provide fodder for research and development, but it is not going to get us to a true open source self-driving car. So, these three major efforts are all interesting and valuable as a means to understand what it takes to craft a self-driving car and yet none will get us toward a working, on-the-road, Level-5 self-driving car. I am willing to put down money on a bet that my predictions will be correct.

Openpilot was started by George Hotz and gained a lot of splash with his efforts in 2016 and 2015. He originally was going to be an upstart to create a self-driving car that would overtake the efforts of Google's Waymo, Tesla, and everyone else in the self-driving car maker space. He boosted that he could use his hacker skills to produce a self-driving car in a fraction of the time and effort that the big guns were doing so. This bluster was brought to the test when he was questioned by the government about meeting self-driving car regulations, which he then tried to fight by claiming they were trying to squash the little guy. He then shifted his business model and decided to make his efforts open source. He says it was to get out from under the thumb of regulations, while others say that he was going nowhere on his self-driving car efforts and would not have been able to meet his bold claims. His stated hope is to become the Android of self-driving cars via his open source efforts. A laudable goal and one that could also bring great commercial success, if it can be pulled off.

His approach consists of providing an open source hardware device called Comma Neo, which provides various sensory capabilities for a self-driving car and is based on the use of an Android phone. It is intended to be mounted where your rear-view mirror sits. You can build the device from the specifications provided by Hotz's project at Comma.AI or look at Github. Some have already done so and created attention for example at the Consumer Electronics Show (CES) in Las Vegas at the start of 2017 (see my coverage of the CES show). Supported cars are currently just the Acura ILX 2016 with AcuraWatch Plus and the Honda Civic 2016 Touring Edition.

The mass media press continues to blindly tout this effort by Hotz as being a self-driving car, but even he openly admits that he has not provided something that can turn your car into a self-driving car. The Openpilot software, available at Comma.AI or Github, provides a lane keeping assist and an adaptive cruise control capability. This not the same as a Level-5 self-driving car. Not even close. They urge that drivers realize that the driver of the car still has the responsibility for driving the car. He defends his open source capabilities as being on par with what Tesla has been providing, and so in that sense one can certainly understand his claims. The mass media press has been as wrong about what Tesla's cars can do as they have been about what self-driving cars are all about.

Udacity is known for wanting to democratize education. They launched their self-driving car "Nanodegree" certificate program to help educate engineers on what it takes to create a self-driving car. Via the use of hundreds or perhaps even thousands of students around the world, they offer an educational program that aims to also produce an open source self-driving car. According to Udacity, since programmers can contribute to applications like Linux and Apache, why not also contribute toward the future of automotive technology too. Opting to buy a 2016 Lincoln MKZ, Udacity has outfitted their one car with some Velodyne VLP-16 LIDARS (see my piece on LIDAR technology), a Delphi radar unit, cameras by Point Grey Blackfly, and other components.

Taking a novel approach to this effort, Udacity has been issuing contests or challenges to get students to contribute source code to the open source project. Aiming at a Level-4 self-driving car, this effort acknowledges that it is not striving for a Level-5 at this time. The first contest consisted of asking students to design a mount for the Udacity provided cameras. Doing so would reduce the noise in the data collected from the cameras, which otherwise were susceptible to the bumpy motions of the car. The next challenge consists of using a neural network for deep learning to predict steering angles. This is all great stuff, but I think you can see that it is like trying to build a self-driving car one itty bitty piece at a time, and doing so by hit-and-miss of whomever happens to want to contribute to the effort. As I say, a wonderful educational experience and goal, but not the likely way to actually produce a self-driving car anytime soon.

Autoware is an academic effort aiming toward open source for a self-driving car, and the project is being led by researchers at Nagoya University and Nagasaki University in Japan. They have chosen to use a ZMP Robo Car that is based on the Toyota Prius. Considered a prototype system, it uses Velodyne LIDAR sensors, Point Grey Ladybug and Grasshopper cameras, Javad RTK sensors for GPS info, and so on. In many respects, this is really more about advancing algorithms for autonomous driving, rather than producing a commercial product that can be sold into the marketplace.

Why am I so seemingly doubtful about anyone being able to successfully bring to fruition an open source version of self-driving car? My reasons are manifold.

First, there is an "arms race" effort now underway to get us to a true self-driving car. You can only compete in that arms race by having incredible focus and determination. Most open source projects tend to be lackadaisical. Those that want to contribute do so, and often are just doing it as a side hobby. Trying to move forward as rapidly as possible on a new innovation does not occur by happenstance.

Second, this is a life-or-death kind of open source project. Most open source projects involve aspects that aren't going to kill you. The source code that controls a multi-ton car or truck has the potential to harm you and others around you. Are you really willing to entrust your self-driving car to some open sourced software that had contributors by anyone that wanted to do so? Imagine if you knew that the braking system for the self-driving car was written by a teenager that wrote the code while also doing their algebra homework in high school.

Third, related to the life-or-death topic, the open source software for a self-driving car must have in-depth attention to safety. If you look at the average programmer and how they code software, safety is usually the last on their list of considerations. Most programmers don't know how to code for safety. They tend to disregard safety issues. The focus is usually to get the "meat" of the system done, and then come back around later on, if they have time, and add some code for safety purposes. For a self-driving car, this is the opposite of what should take place. Safety needs to be at the core, and everything else is added around it.

Fourth, the amount of software needed to fully provide a true self-driving car is huge. Efforts like Openpilot are only scratching the surface of what a self-driving car does. Doing a lane following approach is extremely simple in comparison to the full features of a proper self-driving car. The magnitude of the software, and the complexity, will make it hard and likely futile to have volunteers around the world that can put this together. You need a focused and master minded organized collective to do this.

Fifth, the money to be made right now is for software engineers that have self-driving car software skills to be working at the known auto makers and for-money research outfits. Finding skilled software developers to do self-driving car software of any kind, whether open source or not, can be nearly impossible. The ones that are doing open source tend to be wanna be's, rather than actual working and professional software developers for self-driving cars. Those with the right skills are already working 50 to 60 hours per week at Waymo, Uber, Tesla, Ford, Nissan, and so on. They don't have the bandwidth to be putting effort toward a free-oriented open source project.

If I were you, I wouldn't bet on seeing a self-driving car that was built via open source. Even if it was somehow accomplished, I would have serious doubts about being a passenger in such a car. Though open source is a wonderful concept and at times a beneficial contribution to society, the notion of open source for a commercial version of a self-driving car is doubtful. I am sure we'll have various research oriented open source instances for self-driving cars, and in fact many of those might spring forth new innovations in the self-driving car realm. For those reasons, yes, please do continue the open source efforts. We can use whatever venue possible to push ahead on self-driving car technology.

.

CHAPTER 8

CATASTROPHIC CYBER-HACKING OF SELF-DRIVING CARS

CHAPTER 8

CATASTROPIC CYBER-HACKING OF SELF-DRIVING CARS

In a few years, you'll be enjoying a leisurely drive in your self-driving car. Without having to watch the road, you'll be sipping your brandy as a passenger in your own car and will leave the bothersome chore of driving to AI. Not a care in the world. Well, except for the fact that your self-driving car might be susceptible to cyber hacking. Imagine if your car suddenly "decided" to veer off-course and took you into a blind alley where masked thugs were ready to drag you out of your vehicle and rob you (they not only directed the car to their location, they also forced it to unlock the doors and open them so they could more easily grab you). Or, suppose "just for fun" someone decided to convince your self-driving car to go straight off a cliff. None of these scenarios seems attractive, and yet they all are potentially possible. The key to preventing these calamities is to make sure that self-driving cars have topnotch airtight computer security.

I can't say for sure that self-driving cars will indeed have tough-as-nails computer security. Right now, the security side of self-driving cars is barely getting much attention. In an effort to get self-driving cars to actually be viable, most of the self-driving car makers are putting the bulk of their attention into the core fundamentals of making the car drive. Concerns about cyber hacking are way down on the list of priorities. Meanwhile, we daily are made aware of new hacks that enterprising researchers and others are finding with existing human driven cars.

The irony of sorts is that the more sophisticated that self-driving cars become, the greater the chance that a hack can produce catastrophic results.

Why? Simply because the more that the automation can do to control the car, the more readily a hack or hacker can force the car to do something untoward. If you are driving a classic 1920's Model T car, it is nearly impossible to hack it because there isn't any automation on it to be hacked. On the other hand, a fully autonomous Level-5 self-driving car has the potential to do whatever bidding a hack or hackers want to convey, since the AI is in complete control of the operation of the car. A hack can take over the steering, the braking, the acceleration, and even the internal temperature and air conditioning, the radio of the car, the door locks, and anything else that is connected into the controls of the vehicle.

I am guessing that you are wondering how a hacker or a hack could subvert the control of your self-driving car. When I refer to a hack, I am indicating that a malicious program or application has gotten into the controls of your self-driving car, while when I refer to a hacker it means that a human has been able to maliciously take over the control of your car. The human hacker might be standing on the sidewalk as your car goes past and they have a brief moment to access your car (based on a limited range of trying to electronically communicate with your car such as via Bluetooth), or maybe residing in the car next to you on the freeway. Or, the hacker could be hundreds of miles away and they are using the Internet to gain access into your self-driving car.

There are numerous ways to try and usurp the control of your self-driving car. These are the most promising methods: (a) Remote access via the Internet, (b) Remote access locally such as via Bluetooth, (c) Fooling the sensory devices of your self-driving car, (d) Planting a specialized physical device into your self-driving car, (e) Attaching a specialized physical device onto the exterior of your self-driving car, (f) Inserting a backdoor into the self-driving car via the maker of the car. Let's take a look at each of these methods.

I'll start with a recent news story that involved the placement of a physical device into a car, doing so by connecting to the On-Board Diagnostics (OBD) of the car. This was done on a relatively conventional modern car, and offers a real-world example of what can potentially be done to a self-driving car. The case involved a computer security firm that wanted to see if they could take control of a moving car and somehow subvert the car.

As background about today's cars and their technology, we all know that on our dashboards there are so-called "idiot lights" that illuminate to tell us when our gas tank is nearing empty or when the oil is getting low. You might have also heard a TV or radio ad placed by a car mechanic or car repair service that says they can ascertain the error conditions of your car by bringing it into their shop, wherein they can then connect to your car to read the diagnostic codes. Turns out that since 1996, all cars and light trucks sold in the United States must have an under-the-dash portal that allows for the reading of diagnostic codes. A car mechanic or repair shop can plug into that portal and see what error codes the car has experienced. This is handy for doing car repairs.

There are standards for these diagnostic codes. The Diagnostic Trouble Codes (DTC) standard dictates that the error code begins with a letter, namely P for Powertrain, B for Body, C for Chassis, and U for network, followed by a four-digit numeric code. You can easily look-up the code in a chart and then know what errors the car has experienced. Your dashboard pretty much works the same way. It reads the codes and then illuminates a particular icon such as gas getting low icon or a brake pads are worn icon. In some case, the car maker opted to just show a generic indicator such as "car needs service" rather than trying to display the specifics of the numerous possible codes.

There are many companies that now provide a device that you can purchase as a consumer and connect to the OBD portal. These devices, referred to as dongles, connect to the latest version of the OBD, known as OBD2 or OBD-II. Once you've connected the device to your under-the-dash ODB2 portal, the device will retrieve the error codes from your car, storing the codes similar to a USB memory stick would do, and you can then remove the dongle and plug it into your laptop USB port, allowing you to see a readout of the diagnostic codes. More costly dongles have an LED display that shows the error codes directly, thus bypassing the need to remove it and place it into your laptop.

Even more advanced dongles will allow you to communicate to the dongle via your smartphone. Using Bluetooth, the dongle will allow you to connect your smartphone to the dongle. You download an app provided by the company that provided the dongle. The app communicates with the dongle and tells you what it finds out from your car. So far, this is all innocent enough and certainly seems like a handy boon for those that want to know what their car knows.

Here's what the computer security firm recently did. The smartphone app communicates with the dongle and tries to make a secure connection so that no one else can intervene. Using a brute force technique, the computer security firm found the secret PIN and was able to connect to the dongle, via Bluetooth, and masquerade as though they were the person that had the proper smartphone app that was supposed to be able to communicate with the dongle.

Your first thought might be that it really doesn't seem like much of a hack since all that they can do is read the error codes of the car. Big deal, you say. Unfortunately, there is something about the OBD portal that you need to know. Not only can the ODB portal obtain info from the automation of the car, but it can also convey information into the automation of the car, including the potential to reprogram aspects of the car. Yikes! That's right, built into every car since 1996 as sold in the United States, there is a handy little way to sneak into the automation of your car.

This is known as "security breach through obscurity" meaning that most people have no idea that the OBD is a two-way street, so to speak, meaning that it can read and it also can write into the automation of the car. Only those within the car industry usually know that this is possible. Of course, any determined car hacker readily knows about this. Usually, there isn't an easy way to get direct access to the OBD portal in your car, since the hacker would need to break into your car to try and reach under-the-dash and connect to the portal. Voila, you have made it easy by connecting the dongle and making it available via remote Bluetooth. Your actions have handed the control of your car over to someone maliciously wanting to take over your car and do so from outside of your car.

In the case of the computer security researchers, they were able to inject malicious messages into the car. They had a human start the car and drive the car for a distance, and then suddenly told the car via their own smartphone app and into the dongle and through the OBD that the car engine should shut down. The car happily obliged. Imagine if you had been in the car. The car was zooming along and all of a sudden for no apparent reason the engine stops. This could have led to a car accident and possible deaths. For the computer security research firm, they did this as an exercise to show what is possible, and no one was actually harmed in the act of proving that this was possible. The company that makes the dongle, Bosch Drivelog Connector, quickly implemented a fix, and pointed out that the hacker would have needed to be within Bluetooth range to exploit this hole.

You might also think that you can avoid this kind of catastrophe by simply not installing a dongle onto your car's OBD. Let's move forward in time and think about this. Suppose you have a self-driving car. You might decide to let others use your self-driving car when you don't need to use it, acting kind of like your own version of Uber and trying to pick-up some extra dough by essentially renting out your car. The person using your car could put that dongle onto the OBD. Some say that you can just put tape over the portal and thus stop someone from using this exploit, or maybe putting some other locking mechanism there. Yes, these are possibilities, each with their own vulnerabilities, and we'll be seeing more about this once self-driving cars come to fruition.

Currently, some insurance companies offer incentives to human drivers to plug a dongle into their OBD. A car insurance company might offer discounted rates to human drivers that always stay within the speed limit and that don't do any harsh braking. People are willing to provide this info to the insurance companies in order to get a break on their car insurance premiums. Companies that have a fleet of cars or trucks also use these dongles, doing so to catch their drivers when they drive erratically, or sometimes do so to detect whether their drivers are taking side trips rather than driving directly to their destinations. The point is that the OBD and the dongles are here and now, and unlikely to be stricken from modern cars. We are going to have them on self-driving cars, for sure.

Modern cars have a Controller Area Network (CAN) which is a small network within the car, allowing the various electronic devices to communicate with each other. There are Engine Control Units (ECU's) used for the various components of the car, such as for steering, for the braking, for the accelerator, for the engine, and so on. The ECU's communicate via the CAN. Via the ODB, you can get into the middle of the messages going back-and-forth on this CAN network. Think of it like your WiFi at home, and suppose that someone else jumped onto your WiFi. They could read the messages of your home mobile devices and laptops. They could also take control of your home printer, and your home lights or other Internet of Things devices that are connected into your WiFi.

As mentioned, putting something inside your car to take control is just one of many ways to maliciously subvert the automation of your car. Another method involves fooling the sensors on your car.

In a famous example demonstrated in 2016, researchers were able to fool the Tesla autopilot sensors by using off-the-shelf emitting devices that sent either visual images, sounds, or radio waves to a Tesla car. The Tesla could be drenched in sensory overload that would prevent the self-driving features of the car from being able to discern what is going on. This is a jammer. Or, it could make the sensors believe an object was in front of the car, such as another car, when there wasn't another car there at all. This is a ghost maker. Admittedly, all of these tests were done in a very constrained environment without the car actually moving along the road, and so one can criticize the tests as being overly academic. Nonetheless, it shows the kind of potential that a malicious hacker could try.

A few years ago, there was the case of security researchers that remotely took control of a Jeep Cherokee while it was on-the-road. They did this via an Internet connection into the car. They were able to remotely turn the steering wheel for the Jeep Cherokee as though it was trying to park the car, even though it was zooming ahead at 80 miles per hour. In another test with a different brand of car, they were able to convince a Toyota Prius's collision avoidance system to suddenly apply its brakes, causing it to come to an undesired rapid stop. In each case, they were able to exploit the automation of the car. The more the automation can do, the more they could take over control of the car. Remember that self-driving cars will be chock full of automation and everything on the car will be controlled by automation.

Some worry that the increasing use of advanced entertainment systems in cars is opening an additional can of worms too. The more that your car can do with the Internet, the more chances that a malicious hacker can get electronically into your car. Consumers are clamoring that they want their cars to have WiFi. Consumers want their cars to allow them to cruise the Internet, while cruising on the open highway. Cars are becoming viable targets for Internet attacks, doing so at the urging in a sense of consumers that want their cars to be Internet enabled.

Should we become luddites and insist that no more automation should be allowed into our cars? Should we refuse to ride in self-driving cars? I don't think these are especially viable options. Automation is coming. Self-driving cars are coming. The tide is rising and nothing is going to stop it. That being said, the moment that we being to see real-world instances of self-driving cars that are taken over by hackers, you can bet that's when there will be a hue and cry about cyber security for our cars.

To-date, we've not had any big moments of cars getting hacked and something terrible occurring. It is like earthquakes. Until a massive earthquake happens, we are not thinking about earthquake preparedness. I say that we need to be thinking more seriously about computer security for our cars, now. Especially for self-driving cars as they will be the most vulnerable to allowing malicious control to wreak havoc. We need to yell loudly and implore the self-driving car makers to elevate the importance of computer security.

We also need the AI of the self-driving cars to realize when something malicious is taking place. The AI can be watching over the car and trying to not only control the car, but also trying to detect when something is amiss. The AI though is also a two-way street, since we will soon have hackers that try to trick the AI into doing something malicious. It's going to be a cat-and-mouse game. And involve life-and-death consequences. Block the hackers. Sell the self-driving cars.

CHAPTER 9

CONSPICUITY

FOR

SELF-DRIVING CARS

CHAPTER 9

CONSPICUITY FOR
SELF-DRIVING CARS

Have you gone to the mountains for a hiking trip and ever been offered advice about how to handle an encounter with a bear?

There are two schools of thought about dealing with bears. One approach involves being as loud and obnoxious as you can be, if you encounter a bear. This includes yelling forcefully at the bear, raising your arms above your head, waving your arms back-and-forth, and trying to be as aggressive looking and sounding as you can be. Some even say that you should pick-up a small child (if they happen to be handy and are your child), and hold the child up to make you look larger and fiercer. Or, you might instead open your coat and spread it out to look larger, along with standing as tall as you can and possibly even standing on a tree stump to look taller.

That's the "being conspicuous" school-of-thought about dealing with bears. Meanwhile, there are some that say you should take the opposite tack. You should avoid being aggressive. Stand still. Keep your arms pinned to your side. Don't spread your legs and instead keep them tightly close together. Make no direct eye contact with the bear. No screaming, no yelling, no noises at all. This is the "being inconspicuous" approach to bear interaction.

Which approach should you use? The answer is that it all depends. If you have come upon a bear and it is threatened by you, for example if its cubs are nearby, in that context you might be better off with the conspicuous way of interacting with the bear. On the other hand, suppose that you are crossing a stream and there is a bear that is near the water and it happens to see you. Assuming that there is nothing threatening going on, you probably would be wiser to use the inconspicuous method. You would act almost like you hadn't seen the bear and just quietly continue on your journey.

What does this have to do with self-driving cars? The answer is simple and actually very telling. We need to be enabling self-driving cars with the right kinds of AI-directed conspicuity.

At our Cybernetics Self-Driving Car Lab, we are one of the few self-driving car software makers that is delving into conspicuity. It is something that almost none of the other self-driving car makers are doing anything about. I'd say they are missing the boat.

What is conspicuity for self-driving cars? It is the proper and appropriate utilization of the various ways that a self-driving car can appear either conspicuous or inconspicuous. Notice that we are including being conspicuous or inconspicuous. Many get derailed on this topic by only considering the act of being conspicuous and fail to also consider the other side of the coin, namely being inconspicuous.

Let's take an example of being conspicuous while driving a car. I was driving down Pacific Coast Highway the other morning, it was early in the morning and the sun had not yet risen. In addition to the darkness, there was a dense coat of fog too. Visibility was very poor. Any car ahead of me was pretty much swallowed into the fog if I was more than a half dozen car lengths behind it. I am sure that cars behind me were having a hard time seeing my car too. All in all, this is a pretty dangerous situation. Suppose the car ahead of me suddenly slams on their brakes, I'd have little reaction time and would likely ram into them. Suppose there was debris on the roadway, I'd likely not see it until running over it. Etc.

Some cars were being inconspicuous. By this I mean that they had no headlights on, and they were silently moving along at 55 miles per hour like a hidden shark in the sea. This was scary for them and the other cars. Fortunately, most of the cars did turn on their headlights, increasing their conspicuousness. They were more readily visible than were the cars without headlights on. The cars that wanted to be more conspicuous were driving more cautiously too, often tapping their brake lights, which was a kind of subtle but obvious signal to the car directly behind them. Basically, the driver was saying to cars behind them that they should be driving with caution and the easiest means to do so was by repeatedly tapping their brakes to illuminate their rear brake lights.

I opted to also use the conspicuous methods. In fact, I went even further and was occasionally using my car horn, doing a light tap of the horn. This provided another sensory clue, besides the visual clues of the headlights and brake light. By using sound, I hoped to be even more conspicuous.

One car even turned on its emergency flashers, even though it wasn't stopped by the side of the road. It was still driving, but now driving real slowly and even slightly swerving right and left in the lane. This driver seemed to be wanting to prevent those speed demons that were driving like it was a perfectly sunny day from zooming around them and possibly getting into an accident up ahead. This was not necessarily for the benefit of the speed demon, but more so for the driver that didn't want the speed demon to create an accident and then have that driver get mired into it.

We should expect that our self-driving cars will be able to discern when to use conspicuity. The AI should be gauging the nature of the driving situation and opt to either be conspicuous or inconspicuous, depending upon what is most sensible for the given circumstance. As mentioned, few of the self-driving car makers are thinking about this, let alone developing the AI for it. They are assuming that whatever conspicuity is needed will be done by the human occupants that are in the self-driving car. This though does not make a lot of sense.

If the self-driving car is a level 5 (see my piece about the Richter scale for self-driving cars), we would by definition assert that the car must be completely driven by the AI without any needed human intervention. Having a human occupant have to turn on headlights, tap brake lights, sound horns, these are all actions we expect of a driver, not of a passenger. Furthermore, the level 5 cars that are being envisioned won't necessarily even provide a means for a human occupant to invoke those aspects, such as not having access to the brakes or not having access to the horn. This is something that needs to be reconsidered, by the way, and a future developers and researchers need to address.

For a level 0 to level 4 car, there is a human driver that is expected to pick-up the slack of when the self-driving car cannot figure out what to do. In those instances, the other self-driving car makers are just assuming that the human will take care of turning on or off the headlights (other than when a rather "dumb" sensor realizes it is dark outside), or turning on the emergency flashers, or using the horn. Though this is going to be physically possible to have the human driver do this, I think it puts a burden onto the human driver that we could use the AI to aid.

Please note that I am not saying that we would prevent the human driver from doing those actions, and I would advocate they should be able to do so, but instead saying that we should rightfully expect that the self-driving car will "know" when to use those conspicuity approaches and then use then when needed. Otherwise, the AI is missing out on a vital part of the driving task.

Some pundits will argue that conspicuity is not a vital part of the driving task. They would say that driving the car has little to do with the headlights, the emergency flashers, the horn, etc. They would say these are aspects for humans and that a self-driving car doesn't need to care about humans. These utopian world pundits are confused. They think that all cars on the road will be self-driving cars. Those self-driving cars will communicate via V2V (vehicle-to-vehicle) communications, and the days of using a horn on a car will fall into the past. Wake-up! That's years and years away. For quite some time we will be faced with a mixture of self-driving cars and human driven cars. Self-driving cars must be able to interact with and understand the behavior of human driven cars.

A human driver is apt to notice another car, whether it is a human driven car or a self-driving car, if that car is being conspicuous. My example of driving in the fog is a handy illustration of this. A self-driving car in the fog would normally want to be as conspicuous as it can, alerting other cars to its presence. This might involve not only having headlights on, but also purposely tapping the brakes to illuminate the brake lights. AI developers don't get that idea at first, in that they think the only reason to tap the brakes is because you are trying to slow down the car. That's one aspect of brakes. Another is that we currently use rear brake lights to warn drivers behind us that we are using our brakes. You can use that warning system for another purpose, not necessarily because you are going slower, but just to visually jolt the driver behind you with the quickly flashing brake lights.

Some purists would say that with self-driving cars we won't need brake lights anymore. The radar and other sensors will detect that the car ahead is slowing down, i.e. using its brakes. Well, that's decades away before we see cars abandoning rear brake lights. They are here, they are here to stay. Human drivers know that they can use the brake lights for more than just braking. Same with the horn. Purists say that we won't have horns in cars anymore, no need for them in an all self-driving car era. Again, we're got horns and we're going to keep with horns for the foreseeable future.

Just like we discussed that when confronting a bear that sometimes it is best to become conspicuous, so too is the same for a self-driving car. Besides my example of being in the fog, let's look at some additional examples. I was driving on a curving road in the mountains. As you came to a curve, you could not see around the bend. The road was very narrow. To my right was the mountain, and to my left was a sheer cliff. There were other cars coming down the hill, while I was driving up it. Some of those cars were doing a lousy job of making the bends, and would swerve over into the opposing lane as they did so. This was a situation waiting for something really bad to happen.

I used my headlights by switching from low bean to high beam, which cast a bright light across the curve and helped to warn an oncoming driver that there must be someone else coming around the curve. I used my horn as I went into the curve, in hopes that the other driver might here my car coming. Would a self-driving car do this? It certainly could, and it certainly should. But, if the AI has not been trained to do this or developed to do it, then the human driver or human occupant has to fend for themselves.

Some of the ways for the AI to make the self-driving car more conspicuous include:

- Use of emergency flashers
- Horn with a light touch
- Horn full on
- Pumping the brake lights
- Headlights
- Low beam and high beam of the headlights
- Turning headlights on and off repeatedly
- Weaving
- Slowing/speeding up
- Use of windshield wipers
- Use of spray from windshield wipers
- Etc.

Each of the above should be used sparingly and only when appropriate. Also, they can be used in combination, such as my story about driving on the curving mountainous road and using both the headlights and the horn. In the future, some are predicting that self-driving cars will be outfitted with external advertising displays and be like driving billboards. If so, that's another aspect that could be used to be conspicuous, by displaying messages or indications on that billboard capability.

The self-driving car could even potentially engage the use of the occupants of the car to help the self-driving car appear more conspicuous. I was driving recently during prom week, and there were cars of high schoolers that had their windows rolled down on the cars and were yelling and screaming, and their arms were protruding outside of the car and they were making quite a commotion, having a real party as they drove on their way to the prom. Presumably, a self-driving car could leverage the human occupants by asking them to do something like this, when needed, and therefore make the self-driving car even more conspicuous on the roadway.

So far, we've discussed having the self-driving car look conspicuous. Would it ever want to be inconspicuous? Here's an example. Some say that drunk drivers often aim at other cars on the roadway that are conspicuous. If your car has become disabled and you are stopped on the side of the freeway, some believe that you should make your car conspicuous so that other drivers will avoid hitting your stopped car. Others say that the drunk drivers, those of whom are most apt to hit your disabled car, are actually attracted to a stopped car if it is showing flashing emergency lights or otherwise readily visible. In their drunken state, they are drawn to it, like a moth to a bright light.

If you believe it is better to remain inconspicuous in that circumstance, you'd want your self-driving car to be inconspicuous. I say this because some self-driving car makers are assuming that if your car becomes disabled, you would always want it to be as visible as possible. Not necessarily the case. You might want your car to blend in. You might want your car to be hidden rather than being an attractor.

Self-driving cars not only need to know when and how to best use these conspicuity aspects, they also need to know how to interpret conspicuity that is being utilized by other cars. If a self-driving car comes upon a human driven car that is honking its horn, will the self-driving car even know that's happening? Few of the self-driving car makers are outfitting audio pick-up capabilities onto their self-driving cars. Even if such a sensor is available, the AI needs to determine what is the nature of the sound, what does the sound mean in the situation itself, and what action needs to be taken (see my piece on emergency vehicles in which I discuss sound there too).

We know that when we encounter bears that sometimes it is better to be conspicuous rather than inconspicuous, while other times it is the other way around. Self-driving cars need to know how to leverage their ability to be conspicuous and/or inconspicuous in everyday traffic situations and also in more unique one-off driving tasks. The conspicuity of the capabilities of the car, and the situational awareness are all aspects that the AI must consider. It might seem like a minor thing to most self-driving car makers, but when you have self-driving cars interacting with human driven cars and with other self-driving cars, they are doing a dance that involves showing to each other what is happening on the roadway. Having a self-driving car that is oblivious to conspicuity puts it at a disadvantage on the roads, and furthermore can cause it to either increase the odds of an accident or at least not be as aware of a potential accident that could have been avoided by being more conspicuous. Self-driving cars need to know how to actively participate in the daily dance of traffic.

CHAPTER 10

ACCIDENT SCENE

TRAVERSAL

BY SELF-DRIVING CARS

CHAPTER 10

ACCIDENT SCENE TRAVERSAL
BY SELF-DRIVING CARS

Yesterday, I was driving on the freeway and the traffic was especially bogged down. Most mornings the traffic is slow, but on this occasion, it was really slow, pure stop-and-go kind of driving. Here in Southern California you never can predict what seems to cause traffic patterns to change. Sometimes you guess that there must be an accident up ahead and yet you end-up never seeing any indication that an accident was keeping traffic bottled up. Other times you eventually crawl up upon an accident scene and kind of think, aha, I knew that's what was making me get late to work today. This might seem callous since our first thoughts should go toward whomever was involved in the accident and hoping that they are safe, but with the high volume of accidents we have it is possible to become numb to the nature of accidents and just perceive them as irritating stoppages when you've got to get to someplace on time.

In this case, I did eventually crawl up upon the accident scene. At first, I could just barely see up ahead. From a distance of maybe a quarter mile away of the accident, I could see that there were some emergency vehicles on the freeway, which had flashing lights on. They were tall enough to standout over the cars of traffic. They were stopped on the freeway. They were askew and parked at odd angles, occupying the leftmost two lanes of the freeway. The car traffic itself was like water that flows in whatever direction provides fluidity, and was gradually flowing to the right of the accident scene. This meant that roughly five lanes of traffic were trying to narrow over into about two lanes that were the only way to make your way around the accident scene. Thus, the car traffic was constricted by having to squeeze down into just two lanes, slowing everything down, plus the drivers were gawking at the accident scene and so that too slowed traffic even further.

After seemingly forever, I finally also managed to squeeze over into the rightmost lanes. I had been in the leftmost lane and so it was quite a chore to get toward the right lanes. Even though I had my turn indicator blinker on, nobody in the other lanes wanted to let anyone into the rightmost lanes. It is a cruel world out there on the freeways and often no civility about letting others into your lane. For a circumstance like this, each car was edging forward and wanting to get through the morass as soon as possible, so they weren't interested in letting other cars get over or get ahead of them. At times, some cars tried to force themselves over into the rightmost lanes, doing so an inch at a time and there were "bumper wars" of cars that dare to get within a fraction of an inch of another car, trying to push their way into the next lane over from them and the other cars were desperately and doggedly trying to keep them out.

When my turn came to be in those two scrawny lanes, I then could see the accident scene clearly as I slowly drove past it. The emergency vehicles had formed a kind of cocoon around a motorcycle and a motorcyclist that were both splayed onto the freeway asphalt. There was a medic tending to the motorcyclist. Police were standing nearby and seemed to be taking notes about the accident scene. An ambulance was waiting to take the motorcyclist to the nearest hospital. A fire truck was there, serving to help block the freeway traffic and create the cocoon, and often is one of the first responding emergency vehicles. This is partially due to the aspect that there are sometimes fires that erupt from a car accident and the fire department needs to get there to put out the fire, or prevent one from starting since there is also usually fuel spilled onto the freeway that can easily get ignited.

Within maybe ten seconds, I had finally driven past the accident itself. I had been in line behind the accident scene for nearly an extra twenty minutes of driving time. Now, finally past it, the traffic was thinned out because of the constricting pattern and accident scene blockage. As such, cars that had squeezed past the accident scene were now gunning their engine and racing ahead at breakneck speeds. It was as though the accident scene was a starting line for an Indy car race and the cars that managed to get past the accident scene were excited to hit the gas and see how fast their cars could accelerate from near zero to the top allowed speeds on the freeway.

Most drivers don't realize that this is actually one of the more dangerous aspects of an accident scene. Namely, traffic post-scene drives much too fast and can recklessly then create another new accident. It is not unusual to have an initial accident that spawns a second accident within about a tenth of a mile ahead of the first accident. This is due to cars that misuse the sudden freedom of an open passage to then speed ahead and end-up colliding with other cars. You can imagine how the drivers that have suffered the long wait of getting up to and past an accident scene are in a state of mind of wanting to get going, and so they throw caution to the wind and just push the accelerator pedal to the floor. They are doing so because they are late as a result of being stalled in the wake of the initial accident, and because they are frustrated that a car that can go 80 miles per hour has only been going 5 miles per hour throughout the accident scene area. This potent combination of stressed out drivers and anxiety of wanting to get going will tend to lead to unsafe driving post-scene and result in another accident.

In our Cybernetics Self-Driving Car Lab, we have been creating AI-based capabilities for self-driving cars that allows self-driving cars to traverse these kinds of accident scenes.

Traversing an accident scene is not as easy as you might at first think it would be. Let's take a look at what a self-driving car needs to do when confronted with an accident scene. Us humans are pretty used to dealing with accident scenes and so it is engrained in our driving practices. If you watch a teenage first-time driver that comes upon an accident scene, you'll see them be unsure of what to do. Most of today's self-driving cars are in the same boat. The self-driving car does not have any special AI-algorithms about accident scene traversal. It tries instead to rely upon overall driving practices, but those overall driving practices are not tuned and honed to the specifics of what occurs in an accident scene. Thus, the need for a specialty component for the AI of the self-driving car, a component that provides particular expertise about accident scenes and how to traverse them.

First, the self-driving car needs to realize that there is an accident up ahead. It can do so by detecting that traffic is slowing down and shifting into a stop-and-go kind of pattern. This is done via the use of the cameras, LIDAR, radar and other sensors that the AI is using to detect car traffic. Of course, traffic that slows down does not necessarily indicate there is an accident up ahead. As I mentioned earlier in this piece, I often find that there wasn't any accident and that the traffic slowed for some other reasons, and so the traffic slowing is just one such potential indicator.

Next, the self-driving car needs to detect that there are emergency vehicles involved. In the case of the motorcyclist that was downed, the flashing lights of the emergency vehicles could be seen from quite a distance away of the accident and can be detected via the cameras on the self-driving car. Also, the emergency vehicles were slightly taller than the rest of the traffic and so they could be picked out of the visual images of the traffic and be matched to images of emergency vehicles by the AI-fusion software. This is similar to say doing facial recognition in Facebook, except matching the images of vehicles to what the cameras on the self-driving car are sending into the AI system that's driving the car.

The AI now has several crucial clues in-hand, including that the traffic has slowed down, there are emergency vehicles ahead, they are parked at askew positions, and they have flashing lights on. This is pretty much a high probability that there is an accident scene there. The AI software is using probabilities to assign the odds of what is taking place on the roadway. This is similar to how humans are "guessing" or estimating what is taking place on the roadways. You don't necessarily know things for sure, and so need to gauge the chances that something is or is not taking place. The self-driving car uses probabilities to make these same kinds of guesses and hunches.

A self-driving car that is not wise to accident scenes might just continue to stay in its lane, let's assume that it was in the leftmost lane as I was, and come forward until it reaches the actual accident scene, not realizing that once it gets there that the freeway is effectively blocked off. Today's self-driving cars would normally then bluntly shove the control of the car back to the human, since it has gotten itself into a pickle that it cannot figure out what to do. Once the human driver took over, presumably the human driver would then get the car over to the right, drive past the accident, and then once past it then could re-engage the self-driving car capabilities. These are what the levels 0 to 4 of self-driving cars tend to do in accident scene traversal, i.e., just hand control to the human, but a level 5 by definition cannot just hand the car over to the human driver. There isn't supposed to be a human driver needed by a level 5. So, a level 5 for sure needs to have some kind of "smarts" about driving accident scenes. It would be handy for this to also exist at the levels less than 5, but for sure it must exist at the level 5.

I realize that there are some self-driving car pundits that will be screaming at me that if we had exclusively self-driving cars on the roadway that this accident scene traversal problem would be "solved" and no need to worry about it. In their view, the utopia of all self-driving cars would also imply that the self-driving cars and their AI is communicating via V2V (vehicle-to-vehicle) and so would orchestrate their own dance about how to handle the accident scene. Self-driving cars would collaborate and let each other over into the rightmost lanes in an orderly and efficient manner. The ones closest to the accident would be telling the other self-driving cars what is taking place. What a wonderful world it will be. If that does actually ever happen, it will be decades and decades from now. I think we'll be living on Mars by that time and so maybe we won't even care about day-to-day freeway traffic by then. The point is that this utopian viewpoint is not going to happen anytime soon and so we do need to have self-driving cars that are working independently of each other and able to individually traverse accident scenes. Period.

Back to the matter at-hand, once the self-driving car suspects that an accident scene is up ahead, it then moves into the specialty realm of how to cope with an accident scene. So, first we needed detection to ascertain that an accident scene is now confronting the self-driving car. Next, the self-driving car and its AI invokes the specialty routines for dealing with traversing of accident scenes. These algorithms begin to undertake the planning needed to traverse the accident scene. Some of these plans are based on AI developers that created templates, while other plans are based on the outcome of machine learning. Via machine learning, the system has identified various kinds of accident scenes, and used tons of data about accident scenes and their traversal to try and identify ways to best traverse an accident scene.

There are a number of key factors that impact what a self-driving car should and should not do when confronted with an accident scene. Has the accident just happened or has it become stabilized? In the case of the downed motorcyclist, it was an accident scene that was greatly stabilized. There were already emergency vehicles there. The emergency vehicles had already made their way to the accident scene and were parked there. They had created a cocoon to protect the scene. The human responders were already walking around on the freeway, rendering aid, and otherwise handling the accident scene.

If an accident has just happened, the accident scene itself will be much more chaotic and less predictable. For example, about a month ago, I saw a motorcycle that hit a car ahead of me on the freeway and he flopped onto the freeway. Traffic was moving along at about 30 miles per hour when this happened. The incident occurred right before my eyes. Cars instantly started to jockey out of their lanes to keep from running over the downed motorcyclist and his downed motorcycle. Some cars weren't even aware that anything had happened. Some cars were stopping to block traffic and try to offer aid to the motorcyclist. This whole scene for me lasted only about 15-20 seconds since I was then past it and the evolving aspects were occurring behind me as I continued to drive. I would have stopped if I thought I could be of assistance, but I could see that many others were already doing so.

Anyway, the point is that this was an accident that had just occurred, and there weren't any emergency vehicles there as yet. There wasn't a protective cocoon setup. There weren't any flashing lights. Etc. A self-driving car needs to be able to detect accident scenes that are evolved over time. There is the it-just-is-happening part of the time continuum, and then the accident scene is stabilized portion, and so on. We classify these into emerging accident, happened accident, stabilizing accident scene, rescue accident scene, recovery accident scene, clean-up recovery scene, and re-opened accident scene. For each of these classifications, we have trained the AI to plan and act accordingly.

Besides the phases or stages of an accident, there are other aspects for the self-driving car to be concerned about. What is the traffic situation? Is there almost no traffic or heavy traffic? This is important since it can either make options available or constrain options as to how the self-driving car should react. If there isn't much traffic, the self-driving car can have more lanes to shift into or other evasive actions to avoid or go around the accident scene. There are also special cases such as a toxic spill, or when there is fire involved.

Here's a harrowing experience that I had one time. I was driving on the freeway and in SoCal we sometimes have brush fires during the hot and dry summer months. Turns out that brush on the side of the freeway had gotten on fire and the smoke was billowing across lanes of traffic. Furthermore, flames were leaping from the side of the freeway and actually threatening to burn cars that were driving past the burning brush. What do you do as a human driver? Would you stop your car before you got to the flames and smoke? Or, would you try to drive at a high speed and kind of scoot through and past the flames and smoke? Some cars were trying the high-speed escape, while others were frantically trying to get into the leftmost lane and come to a stop ahead of the flames and smoke.

This illustrates that the nature of an accident scene can be very dynamic. The self-driving car not only has to consider what it will do, but also what other drivers will do. And, as stated earlier, the self-driving car is going to be having to predict what human drivers are going to do. Will those human drivers that are nearby to the self-driving car going to do something sensible or maybe something wild? The AI cannot rely upon some pre-scripted and canned approach to handling the accident scene. The dynamic and evolving nature of an accident scene requires not only some kind of template but also a capability of judging on-the-fly what to do.

Another consideration is that the self-driving car itself might become part of the accident scene. For example, when I mentioned before that I had seen a motorcyclist get hit, you could argue that I now was part of the accident scene and that I should either stop to render aid or that I should stop to serve as a witness to what happened. Will we expect our self-driving cars to do likewise? In other words, the self-driving car "saw" an accident with its cameras, LIDAR, etc., and so it should potentially stop to provide that info for purposes of analysis of the accident and how it happened. Also, what if the occupants inside the self-driving car also saw the accident? Shouldn't the self-driving car make them available? Or, suppose the human occupants want to stop and render aid, they somehow have to tell the self-driving car to do so (with a level 5 it is still an open question about how the occupants will be communicating with the self-driving car).

I have so far focused on accidents occurring on a freeway, but accidents happen in all kinds of driving contexts. One day, I came upon an accident that had happened in a residential neighborhood and two cars had run into each other. The two cars were completely blocking the road, and there were parked cars at the curbs that further blocked the road. Other cars could not get past this accident scene. As a result, cars would drive up to the accident scene, the human driver would realize they could not get around it, and then they would try to make a U-turn there in the middle of the road. Other cars coming behind them didn't know what was going on. The U-turn cars were then going head-to-head with other unsuspecting cars driving up to the scene. It was a mess.

This is the kind of AI specialty that we need to have in our self-driving cars. Coping with accident scenes must be handled in circumstances involving freeways, highways, city driving, suburbs, and so on. The weather also plays a big role in how to traverse an accident scene, such as whether the road has ice and snow on it. Time of day as to whether it is nighttime or daytime is a significant factor. Whether there is one car involved in an accident, or multiple cars, also plays into this. I was living in Germany and one day saw a pile-up of cars that involved around 40 vehicles that had all hit each other in a crazy domino way.

The severity of the accident is another crucial factor. We have all come upon a simple fender bender, which usually involves two cars that then get off the road and deal with exchanging insurance info. This is quite different from an accident scene where there has been injury or deaths involved. Traversal in an area that has humans injured or dying is something that a self-driving car has to be especially cautious about.

There are also aspects of obeying whatever is taking place at the scene such as when a police officer decides to direct traffic as part of aiding accident scene traversal. I came up to an accident recently and there was a stop sign just before it. A police officer that had stabilized the accident scene was directing traffic. He was motioning for cars to drive through the stop and not come to a stop. In fact, when cars were stopping (because they saw the stop sign and figured they legally had to stop), he got quite irritated as he was purposely wanting to keep traffic flowing and so his motions were overriding the stop sign. Getting a self-driving car to realize that it should ignore a stop sign and instead obey the motions of a police officer is a difficult task. The AI has to be able to visually recognize the officer, it must be able to override its usual rules about stop signs, etc.

There are an estimated 6 million accidents per year in the United

States. The odds are pretty high that on any daily driving journey of any substance that you will likely come upon an accident, whether it is an accident that is just occurring or the aftermath of one that already occurred. Self-driving cars need to know what to do when they come upon an accident scene. For most self-driving cars of today, they just kind of give-up and hand the driving over to the human driver. This is not only dangerous since the human driver has to suddenly become engaged in driving, it also belies the hope of someday getting to a level 5 true self-driving car that does not rely upon having a human driver available. By our developing specialized AI algorithms for self-driving cars that are faced with accident scenes, we are improving the capabilities of self-driving cars. Even if by some miracle we begin to see less accidents once self-driving cars are readily available (though see my debunking of that by my piece on zero accidents due to self-driving cars), there will still be a mixture of human drivers and self-driving cars, and there will still be accidents. Self-driving cars need to know what to do.

.

CHAPTER 11

EMERGENCY VEHICLE

AWARENESS

FOR SELF-DRIVING CARS

CHAPTER 11

EMERGENCY VEHICLE AWARENESS
FOR SELF-DRIVING CARS

It used to be that when you heard the sound of a siren coming from a police car or ambulance or fire truck that all nearby drivers would scurry to pull their cars over to the side of the road. In California (and in most other locales in the United States), it's the law that you must yield the right-of-way to any emergency vehicle that is using a siren or deploying flashing lights. You used to see drivers pull over religiously and without hesitation, but lament that it seems that today's drivers are less apt to abide by this law. Some drivers will speed-up in hopes of somehow racing ahead of the emergency vehicle. Some drivers make a rather feeble attempt to pull over, as though they are quasi-acknowledging the law, but pretty much otherwise are determined to proceed and unwilling to relinquish the road to the emergency vehicle. Whether due to laziness, disdain, confusion, ignorance, or defiance, many drivers aren't as rigorous as they once were about obeying this law.

Of course, these scofflaws are endangering all potential stakeholders, including endangering themselves, the passengers in their car, other drivers and their passengers, and the emergency vehicle with its occupants. By remaining in the midst of the roadway or taking bizarre actions, they can cause the emergency vehicle to have to swerve dangerously to avoid them. Sometimes the emergency vehicle will need to come to crawl to deal with those blocking traffic, and so this endangers too the lives of those that perhaps the emergency vehicle is trying to save, such as an ambulance that is rushing an injured patient to the hospital or a fire truck that is trying to get to a raging fire to rescue people trapped in a burning building. I've asked some of these danger-producing drivers why they don't seem to care about the lives of others and usually they feign innocence. They didn't hear the siren. They didn't see the flashing lights. They heard the siren but didn't think it was anything worth being concerned about. They saw the flashing lights but figured the emergency vehicle would just find a way around their car and so they decided to just let the emergency vehicle driver worry about what to do.

I will get off my high-horse about these inhumane human drivers and now focus instead on the emerging AI-based self-driving cars. What would a self-driving car do when an emergency vehicle approaches? By-and-large, nearly all of the existing self-driving cars are ill-equipped to detect, recognize, and react to an emergency vehicle. Since most of the self-driving cars are at a less than level 5 capability (see my piece about the Richter scale for self-driving cars levels), the self-driving car makers assume that the human driver in the self-driving car will be the one to detect that an emergency vehicle is nearby, and it will be up to the human driver to take over controls of the self-driving car. This is problematic due to the aspect that the human driver in the self-driving car might take over and not take the correct action due to a cognitive "gap" in what is occurring in the driving environment at the moment, or the human driver might not have time to properly react and thus belatedly take over control of the self-driving car.

Imagine if the human driver hears the siren of an approaching ambulance, which is nearing the car at a speed of 60 miles per hour and the car itself is going 30 miles per hour. The human driver detects the siren, mentally calculates that there is something going on nearby, looks around to see if the emergency vehicle can be seen, and suppose they suddenly see it rushing up behind them. Now, this human driver that is in a self-driving car and for which we'll assume that the self-driving car is doing the driving, will need to mentally ascertain the status of their own car, what speed it is going, what direction, what is the other traffic around them, where is the safest spot to pull over, what will happen to other traffic when they try to pull over, and so on. Next, the human driver will need to put their hands on the steering wheel and their feet onto the pedals of the car, and disengage the AI of self-driving car. Finally, the human driver will then need to take the evasive action. All of this often must occur with just a few seconds of hearing the siren or seeing the flashing lights.

It is pretty easy to predict that we're going to have problems when these kinds of situations arise. The human driver will be stressed to make the right decision and maybe make the wrong decision and radically pull to the side of the road. But, this might cause a cascading problem for other drivers, and those cars now suddenly need to do risky maneuvers to get out of the way of the human driver and also of the approaching emergency vehicle. This can become a "game" of bombardment with other cars bumping into each other or otherwise scrambling and scraping or hitting each other. Keep in mind too that the traffic will likely have a mixture of both human driven cars and self-driving cars. This is crucial because it means that the AI of the self-driving cars needs to be able to contend with traffic that radically goes awry when an emergency vehicle situation presents itself.

In our Cybernetics Self-Driving Car Lab we have examined what happens in these kinds of situations.

One scenario involves the AI not knowing that an emergency vehicle is approaching and so is unaware of the circumstances and what is going to arise. This lack of awareness is partially due to the fact that almost none of the self-driving car makers are outfitting their self-driving cars with an audio capturing capability, and thus the self-driving car has no chance to "hear" the sounds of sirens. We have been exploring the use of sound capturing equipment that would be listening for crucial sounds such as a siren. The self-driving cars also don't tend to look for flashing lights that are on an emergency vehicle. We are exploring ways of visually detecting the flashing lights, via interpreting the visual images being captured by cameras on the self-driving car. This is a harder problem than you might think. The emergency vehicle can be at a great distance and so hard to see, the flashing lights can be obscured by other objects and cars that are on the road, etc. If the AI cannot do an early detection about the approaching emergency vehicle, it hampers the chances of the AI being able to take appropriate action, and will again require the human driver to intervene.

Another scenario that comes to play is the reaction of the other cars around the self-driving car. Even if the self-driving car cannot hear the siren and nor detect the flashing lights, it can detect that other cars around it are making unusual maneuvers. In other words, imagine that you are driving a car and suddenly you notice the cars around you are all jockeying to get over to the side of the road. You hopefully are astute enough to deduce that something is happening. Now, you might not be sure that those cars are maneuvering due to an emergency vehicle, and it might be that there is a mighty earthquake shaking the earth or an apocalypse taking place, but at least you are sparked into the realization that something is happening and you should likewise probably do something about it.

The AI of the self-driving car in its simplest form has to figure out how to yield right-of-way to the approaching emergency vehicle. This is the easiest of the steps. What requires even more intellectual punch is to deal with the rapidly evolving situation of other cars also scrambling to get out of the way of the emergency vehicle. In other words, if you only anticipate that your car needs to get over, and if you assume that all other cars stay where they are, that's an unrealistic way to program the self-driving car. You need to assume that all other traffic will be doing something, whether it is an attempt to react to the emergency vehicle or whether it is ignoring or not responding to the emergency vehicle. All circumstances are feasible, involving a mix of both human drivers and self-driving cars, and some that will be reacting dramatically, some that will be reacting mildly, and some that aren't reacting at all.

I have heard some self-driving car makers claim that this act of responding to emergency vehicles is a "non-problem" because they are assuming that soon all vehicles will be equipped with V2V (vehicle-to-vehicle communications), and therefore they are anticipating that the emergency vehicle will transmit a message to the self-driving car that says "get out of the way." I agree that eventually we'll have this kind of communications. It isn't going to be anytime soon. The utopian world of these self-driving car makers is decades away. Not only do the self-driving cars need to get equipped with these V2V capabilities, there will need to be standard protocols established and promulgated about what those messages are and how to convey them. Different self-driving car makers will likely craft their own protocols. The regulatory bodies will eventually weigh-in. Meanwhile, there is also the chance of someone spoofing these protocols and tricking your self-driving car into getting out of the way when they instead are rushing to that nighttime baseball game, and not due to being an emergency vehicle being in an actual emergency situation (see my piece on cybersecurity for self-driving cars).

I have been herein simplifying the situations too by describing the situations as merely getting over to the side of the road when reacting to the emergency vehicle. There are a myriad of other circumstances that need to be considered. For example, one day I was driving on the freeway and a highway patrol car with a siren and flashing lights was in the far left lane of traffic and trying to get ahead of a pack of cars (I was driving in that pack). The highway patrol car came up to where I was driving, and then pulled in front of the cars at my lateral position, and began to weave back-and-forth across all lanes of traffic. If you've never seen this happen, please be aware that this a driving tactic that means that all traffic is to stay behind the highway patrol car. This is something too that we have been teaching our AI self-driving car system to recognize and react to.

Anyway, the highway patrol car starts weaving. Besides having us stay behind his car, the patrolman also began to go slower and slower. This led to all of the traffic to go slower and slower too. Again, this is a common trick, and is being done to create a break in traffic up ahead of the patrol car. Usually, there is something that has landed onto the roadway, some kind of debris, and another patrolman up ahead wants to get out of his car and grab the debris. The patrolman slowing down traffic is creating a break in traffic that will ensure that no cars are speeding toward the other patrolman and he or she can then run out into the freeway to quickly retrieve the debris.

Well, what happened next can be somewhat shocking if you've not seen this happen before. The highway patrol car weaves nearly to a stop, and so I also was coming to a near stop, and then all of sudden the patrolman makes a U-turn in the middle of the freeway and faces the oncoming traffic (which has now come to a complete stop). It was like a gunfighter facing a crowd of gunfighters. Face to face. Somewhat eerie and disconcerting. Had no idea what this was about. A few minutes later, a helicopter appeared overhead. Turns out that they wanted to land the helicopter onto the freeway, doing so to place an injured person into the helicopter and be whisked away to a hospital. Though I was upset that I had to wait and was greatly delayed in getting to work, it is admittedly a rare occasion that you get to see a helicopter land on the freeway. A sight to behold. Naturally, I also was hoping that the injured person would urgently get their needed medical care.

The action of making the U-turn was pretty unusual, though it can and does happen. The weaving and slowing of traffic happens routinely. These are all scenarios that a self-driving car needs to be able to recognize and then intelligently react to. Think of the many other circumstances that can also arise. For example, a motorcade of the mayor or the president, which then requires cars to appropriately act. A funeral procession. A tow truck that is towing a disabled vehicle. A highway patrol car that is pulling over a driver to give them a ticket. A car chase of a wild driver trying to get away from the police (as trivia, you might find of interest that the Southern California area is somewhat considered the "king" of car chases and we have them all the time; the news media loves it and will switch all TV and radio programming over to watching the car chase unfold).

The AI of the self-driving car needs to cope with these situations. We aren't going to have V2V widespread any time soon. And, relying solely on the back-up human driver to take the controls of the self-driving car is a lousy approach. Plus, we'll never get to the true self-driving car, the level 5, until we are able to get the AI to handle the emergency vehicles circumstances. There are other twists too, such as you are not allowed to stop your car in an intersection when trying to react to an emergency vehicle, and so this is another rule that the self-driving car needs to know about. Also, emergency vehicles can and will often use the wrong side of the road to make their way and avoid being slowed down by other cars. This is another tactic that the self-driving car needs to take into account.

On the topic of detecting audio, besides detecting a siren, the self-driving car needs to ascertain how far away the siren is. Is the siren getting closer or going further away? What kind of siren is it? Is it truly of an emergency vehicle or some other kind of siren (notably, where I live, each month they run sirens all around town as part of the monthly tsunami warning system, which even naive human drivers sometimes mistake as an emergency vehicle sounding its alarm). Detecting a siren is more than merely picking the sound out of the cacophony of street sounds. It also requires intelligent analysis. Then, there are other potential sounds too, such as a patrol officer using their loud speaker. Just the other day, I had a patrol officer in their car that was telling cars ahead of it to slow down.

In this case, imagine the complexity of trying to hear the spoken words, interpret the spoken words, assess that they are legitimate commands by an authorized officer of the law, and then act upon what is being spoken. This is many times harder than merely detecting just a siren.

There is very little effort as yet on having AI that can detect, recognize, and respond to emergency vehicles. In our Cybernetics Self-Driving Car Lab, we are pushing the envelope on AI for self-driving cars by establishing system tactics and strategies to cope with emergency vehicles. Using simulations and machine learning, we are improving self-driving car capabilities so that back-up human drivers won't be thrust into the dire throes of having to figure out at the last minute how to take over controls of the car, and also so that we can be heading toward the level 5 self-driving car that can handle these situations all by itself. Next time that you are driving and encounter an emergency vehicle, be thinking about the thinking that is required to deal with an emergency vehicle. Plus, be aware of how complex the situations can be, and how deadly, and also how life saving those moments are, and the crucial nature of intelligent reactions to them.

CHAPTER 12

ARE LEFT-TURNS RIGHT

FOR SELF-DRIVING CARS

CHAPTER 12

ARE LEFT-TURNS RIGHT FOR SELF-DRIVING CARS

I was driving my car the other day and came to an intersection that allowed me to make a left turn, but there wasn't protective pocket and nor was there a green arrow available. Instead, this was a rather harrowing circumstance of occupying a lane that allowed cars to either go straight or make a left turn, and that permitted a left turn once oncoming traffic provided a break significant enough to make the left turn. A car ahead of me was also trying to make this death defying left turn. I could see her inch her car further forward into the intersection and was obviously hopeful that if she wasn't able to make the left turn during the green light that she could at least do so once the intersection went to yellow. The oncoming traffic was streaming continuously and there wasn't any break that she could try to dive into.

The light went to yellow and the oncoming traffic was determined to get as many cars straight through as possible. Finally, the light went entirely to red and there were still two oncoming cars that opted to scream through the intersection at rocket like speeds. The left turning car ahead of me was in for trouble since it couldn't make the left turn yet, and now there was an onslaught of perpendicular traffic that was eager to use their green light to proceed. After some honking of horns and waving of fingers, the left turner made the turn and probably was still shaking from fright and of being touched by the icy grip of the grim reaper.

There are some that say we should ban all left turns. That's right, ban them. According to the National Highway Traffic Safety Association (NHTSA), whenever there is a crash involving cross of paths, it is about half the time involving a left turn, while only about 6 percent of the time does it involve a right turn. New York City says that left-hand turns are about three times as likely to involve an injury or death for pedestrians as do right-hand turns. The NHTSA statistics indicate that over a third of motorcycle fatalities involve a car that was making a left-hand turn that occurred in front of an oncoming motorcycle. Overall, these rather depressing statistics do seem to suggest that left turns are the bane of our existence.

Designers of roads and traffic pathways are urged to avoid creating left turns and there are calls afoot by regulators to reduce the number of left turns in our transportation infrastructure. No left turns would mean that all of these incidents and accidents involving left turns would disappear. No need to fret in those left turn lanes anymore. No need to have a special green arrow to approve making a left turn at an intersection. In theory, we would only make right turns. That's it, the right turns wins out. Go, right turns, go.

An often-cited aspect about the dreaded left turn is that many of the logistics companies abide by the rule-of-thumb to avoid left turns. For example, UPS is widely known for having instituted a practice of avoiding left turns. Keep in mind though that they did not ban entirely left turns. It is an urban myth that some believe that UPS executives have decreed that their drivers are to never make any left turns. This notion is entirely fiction. Instead, UPS uses their specialized GPS mapping system to minimize left turns when appropriate to do so.

What's also interesting about this minimization of left turns is that it is not solely due to the accident rates associated with left turns. According to most studies of left turns, the time you spend waiting to make a left turn is relatively high, and so you are then delayed in getting to your destination and your vehicle uses more fuel. For transport and logistics companies like UPS, time is money, and so is fuel. If they can reduce the amount of time to deliver a package, and reduce fuel consumption, it will make them more profitable.

Why do we care here about left turns? When developing a self-driving car, one question that keeps being raised is whether or not a self-driving car should be making left turns. It might be safer for self-driving cars if they did not make left turns. Safer for the self-driving car and its occupants, and safer for other cars on the road, and safer for pedestrians too. Furthermore, using the UPS example, presumably the self-driving car might get faster to its destination and use less fuel, if it did not use left turns (though the driving practices of delivering packages is not the same as everyday driving patterns).

I've even heard some say that self-driving cars should be forced to never use left turns. A law should be passed that would ban any self-driving car from ever making a left turn, say some alarmists. These extremists even want that the AI of the self-driving should not know how to make a left turn, which then will ensure that the self-driving doesn't inadvertently make a left turn, ever.

Crazy talk! That's right, this is all crazy talk. Regulating self-driving cars to prevent them from making left turns, this is nutty. Purposely omitting the left turn capabilities from the AI of the self-driving car, even nuttier. Left turns are here and will continue to be here for many, many years to come. In fact, if you want to believe the utopian self-driving world of the future, which is when all cars on the road will only be self-driving cars, and these self-driving cars will communicate with each other via V2V (vehicle-to-vehicle communications), we can have left turns aplenty. That's because in this utopian perfect world the self-driving cars will all politely talk with each other and coordinate their movement. Thus, a left turn will be a piece of cake. The ongoing traffic will talk with the self-driving car that is making the left turn, and the oncoming self-driving cars will ensure that a proper break in traffic allows the left turner to proceed without any worry.

But, let's get back to reality. The AI of self-driving car needs to know how to make left turns. Left turns are an essential maneuver in driving a car. Now, this does not mean that the AI needs to always rely upon left turns. Similar to how UPS urges drivers to avoid left turns when feasible, the AI can be programmed to try and avoid left turns that are especially dicey. Based on history of the roads that the self-driving car is driving on, the AI can judge the risks associated with any given left turn and then opt to make the left turn or not. Human drivers also make this same calculation, and often choose to avoid a left turn or do something else about a particularly gnarly left turn.

Here's a left turn example that I encountered just last week. I came up to an intersection that my GPS said I need to make a left turn as part of my path toward my destination. Cars were already quite backed-up and overflowing out of the left turn pocket. These cars protruded out into the normal lanes of traffic. Only about one or at most two cars at a time were able to make the left turn, during the intersection green-yellow-red light cycles. I realized that if I sat in this long line of cars that were awaiting making the left turn that it would take maybe an added ten minutes just to make that one turn.

I looked ahead and saw another left turn just a short distance away. There wasn't any traffic sitting in that left turn lane. So, I drove up sneakily about a quarter block ahead and used that left turn to make my needed turn. Yes, it put me a little away from the street that I was supposed to be on, but with an additional turn I then got onto that street. I am sure that I easily beat the time that would have taken had I stayed in that earlier overly crowded left turn lane.

The point is that yes, I did make a left turn, but used one that was faster and safer to make. Judicious use of left turns is the mantra for any human driver, and likewise should be the mantra for any sophisticated AI that is doing the self-driving of a car. The existing situation surrounding any given left turn should be processed and a determination made about whether to make that left turn or not. Blindly making a left turn simply because the GPS says to make a left turn is not very smart. We want the AI to go beyond the norm of a typical GPS and add some smarts to making turns, especially for left turns that are in bad situations.

We have been analyzing left turns as part of our efforts at our Cybernetic Self-Driving Car Lab and devising self-driving car modules that specialize in dealing with left turns.

What's a bad situation for a left turn?

Here's some clues:

- No left turn pocket
- Left turn restricts the forward flow of traffic
- Left turn at a major intersection
- Lots of traffic involving the left turn
- Nighttime tends to be dicey versus daytime
- Visibility and weather conditions obscuring the roadway
- Left turns known for accidents
- Places where lots of pedestrians are nearby the left turn
- And so on

The roadways are designed to allow for Protected Permitted Left-Turn (PPLT) in certain areas. In theory, the local transportation authority is supposed to be monitoring these left turns and adjust the left turns or remove them if they are dangerously high in rate of accidents. Our system taps into these statistics to also try and gauge how lethal a particular left turn might be. There is also the LTAP/OD, which means to be aware of the Left Turn Access Path (LTAP) and the Opposite Direction (OD) of traffic.

For human drivers, they are taught to follow certain kinds of steps when making a left turn. Experienced drivers tend to do these steps and are not even aware that they are doing so. Though, some experienced drivers have over time opted to neglect the steps and so they are making left turns perhaps more on a hunch than by actually abiding by advised steps. If you watch a teenager learning to drive, you can see the steps since they are often doing them for the first time and make overt actions corresponding to those steps.

Here's the typical steps involved:

- Have the AI move the self-driving car into the left turn lane or hug the center divider line if no left turn lane exists

- Have the self-driving car start signaling before it makes the left turn, which lets traffic around it know the intentions of the AI

- Reduce the self-driving car speed as it comes toward the left turn

- Come to a stop behind the limit line if it cannot in one swoop make the left turn

- Scan the oncoming traffic to identify a break in traffic using radar, cameras, LIDAR

- Gauge the time and distance needed to make the left turn

- Ensure that there will be sufficient clearance regarding oncoming traffic

- Scan for pedestrians and ensure that the turn won't conflict with their movement

- Scan for bicyclists and ensure that the turn won't conflict with their movement

- Scan for motorcyclists that are oncoming and that might conflict with the turn

- Determine the safety factor associated with when to make the turn

- Execute the turn once the safety factor is at an acceptable threshold

- Don't cut the corner on the left turn

- Don't go too soon

- Don't go to late

- During the turn, continue to monitor all sensors and adjust as needed

- Keep the wheels straight prior to making the turn (in case hit from behind)

- Judge whether the car behind is going to try and make the turn too

These approximately twenty steps are just a tip of the iceberg of the AI cognitive effort involved in making a left turn. It needs to anticipate the left turn. It needs to plan for the left turn. It needs to be collecting sensory data and use it to assess the nature of the left turn. It needs to continually adjust to the evolving situation about the left turn. It needs to do re-planning as needed. It needs to execute the left turn. During the execution, it needs to continue collecting sensory data and be ready to adjust the driving action.

Situational awareness is crucial. Is this a left turn in a suburb or in the inner city? Is the road well paved and designated or is it a hidden path? Do the nearby drivers seem to be driving carefully or with abandon? Does the time of day make a difference? Does the day of the week make a difference? What is the volume of traffic? What are the speeds of the traffic? Is it at a controlled intersection? Is it a left turn in the middle of the road? Etc.

This is where collecting lots of self-driving car data is especially handy. If there are hundreds of other self-driving cars that have tried to make that same left turn, the system can use that data. By applying machine learning, it can ascertain the nuances associated with successfully making that left turn. The machine learning might discover that there is a pattern to always going quickly or instead always waiting until the last car traverses past.

There are other twists to the left turn cognitive effort too. Certain kinds of tactics and strategies apply to a left turn from a two-way street onto a two-way street. There are other kinds of tactics and strategies for making a left turn from a two-way street onto a one-way street. Likewise, for a one-way street onto a one-way street, and for a one-way street onto a two-way street.

Most self-driving cars are already able to do left turns in a rudimentary fashion. Tending to be extremely cautious, you can pretty much know when a self-driving car is making a left turn, since it is about as timid as a teenage driver learning to drive. There are human drivers that will "game" a self-driving car and play chicken with it. If you were in an oncoming human driven car and saw that a self-driving car was readying to make a left turn, you could pretty much "know" that the self-driving car is going to wait for you to pass before it opts to make the left turn.

Those squeaky close left turns that human drivers make are not how the self-driving cars have been programmed. Instead, most of the self-driving cars are programmed to only make the left turn when it seems abundantly clear that the left turn can be made. Some believe that we will gradually see the self-driving cars get more akin to those squeaky close driving aspects by having used their machine learning to refine making left turns. In essence, if a given left turn has been undertaken thousands of times by the collective of other self-driving cars, then any particular self-driving car can use the pattern and optimize for traversing that left turn.

Let's at least dispense with the idea that left turns should never be done by self-driving cars. This is going to continue to come up and I am expecting that "journalists" that don't know much about self-driving cars are going to wring their hands and argue for doing away with left turns by self-driving cars. I would even predict that we'll soon be having an accident involving a self-driving car while making a left turn, and this will get the mass media all charged up about left turns. Regulators that want to look good to their constituents might jump on the "no left turns for self-driving cars" bandwagon. I say, don't toss out the baby with the bath water.

Making left turns is part of the real-world of driving. We need to ensure that self-driving cars can make left turns. We need to continuously improve how self-driving cars make left turns, and strive to aim for as much safety as we can. No matter how safe we aim, in the end, the self-driving cars are mixing with human driven cars and the combined unpredictable nature of the real-world is going to have self-driving cars get into accidents. The utopian world is not here yet.

CHAPTER 13

GOING BLIND: WHEN SENSORS GO BAD ON SELF-DRIVING CARS

CHAPTER 13

GOING BLIND: WHEN SENSORS GO BAD ON SELF-DRIVING CARS

I was in a hurry the other day and jumped into my car to try and rocket across town for an important appointment. When I started the engine, suddenly my "idiot lights" dashboard lit up and indicated that I had a low tire pressure. I've seen this before and from time-to-time have had a tire that was a few pounds low after having driven up to the Bay Area from Los Angeles. In this case, I was taken aback because the dashboard indicated that all four tires were at low pressure. My first thought was that this was impossible. How could all four tires be low at the same moment in time? Then, after a fleeting thought that maybe someone slashed all four tires, I got out of the car to take a look at them. They appeared to be intact. I luckily had a tire gauge in my car and used it to measure the amount of air in the tires. Seemed like they were properly inflated.

I opted to turn off the engine and start the car again. The four tires still showed as though they were at low pressure. This was becoming irritating and frustrating, and of course was taking place just when I was in a hurry to get someplace. Murphy's law strikes! I decided that since the tires are run-flat tires that allow you to drive when they go flat, I would go ahead and slowly ease out of the parking lot and see what happens. I proceeded like a timid driver and made my way inches at a time toward the opening to the street. One by one, the low tire pressure sensor dashboard lights went out, suggesting that I was now OK with my tires.

I am sure we have all had circumstances whereby a sensor in the car goes bad or sometimes is momentarily faulty. We expect this aspect of any kind of mechanical device on our cars. Our headlights sometimes fail and need to be replaced. Our brakes get worn after a while and the brake pads need to be replaced. No car is perfect. No car is maintenance free. For some people, they are "lucky" and seem to never have anything go wrong on their car. Other people get a "lemon" of a car that seems to be unlucky and always has something going wrong. We generally expect that an older car is going to have more problems and maintenance. We generally assume that a cheaper car is going to have more problems and more maintenance than an expensive car. We also expect that an expensive car will likely have expensive maintenance whenever maintenance is required. These are the laws of nature about sensors and devices on our cars that can falter or fail.

What about self-driving cars? You don't hear much about sensors going bad on self-driving cars. But, that's for a very apparent reason. Self-driving cars right now are like well-cared-for high-end Nascar racing cars. Teams of engineers fret about any little blip or blemish on their precious self-driving cars. The sensors on these prototype cars are costly and kept in really good shape. If a sensor happens to become faulty or go bad, an engineer quickly removes the offending item and replaces it with a brand new one. Realizing that the self-driving car makers are spending millions upon millions of dollars to develop and perfect self-driving cars, you can bet that any sensor that goes bad is going to instantly get kicked out and replaced by a shiny new one.

This makes sense when you are trying to develop something new and exciting. Think though about what will happen once self-driving cars are actually on-the-roads and doing their thing each and every day. Eventually, we are going to have everyday self-driving cars that are going to be subject to the same vagaries as our everyday cars today. The brakes are going to wear out, the headlight beams will go out, and the specialized sensors such as the cameras, the LIDAR, and the radar sensors will all ultimately have some kind of failure over their lifetimes. In fact, you could predict that the faults and issues of sensors is going to be even more heightened on self-driving cars because they are chock full of those sensors. There might be a dozen cameras, another dozen radar sensors, one or two LIDAR systems, and so on.

Welcome to a new world of sensor mania in the realm of self-driving cars. For those that make replacement car parts and do automotive maintenance, this actually could be a blessing in disguise.

Imagine hundreds of millions of cars with then tens of hundreds of millions of sensors, all of which will be statistically failing at one time or another. Bonanza! The odds are too that these sensors at first won't be easily attached or embedded into the car in some simple fashion. More than likely, trying to replace these sensors is going to require doing all sorts of surgery on the car to get them out and replaced. Furthermore, once you remove and replace the sensor, the amount of testing to make sure that the new sensor is working properly will take added labor time. Those dollars are racking up.

Nobody wants to utter these aspects when discussing self-driving cars. Instead, we are told to think about a utopia of these self-driving cars whisking us all around town and the humans don't have a care in the world. Have you ever seen a bus that is parked on the side of the road because it had a failure of some kind? Ever been on a subway that slowed down or stopped because of some kind of systems problem or failure? Mass transit systems have these kinds of faults and failures all the time. Our autonomous AI-led self-driving cars are just as susceptible to breakdowns, and as mentioned even more so due to the plethora of gadgets and gizmos that enable the car to do its self-driving.

Besides the obviousness of the hardware sensors, we must also consider that these upcoming self-driving cars are going to have boatloads of computer processors on-board, which is what makes the AI aspects possible. Memory in those chips can go bad, the processors themselves can wear out or bust, and other various hardware maladies can occur. So far, I've only emphasized the hardware, but we need to think about the software too. Suppose there is a hidden bug in the self-driving car software. Some self-driving car makers also are interconnecting their self-driving cars by using the Internet, including so-called over-the-air software updates. The hardware that allows these interconnections can go bad, plus the software updates pushed into the self-driving car can get pushed incorrectly or get load improperly.

I hope this doesn't burst that self-driving car utopia that some are dreaming about. Realistically, we need to anticipate that stuff will go wrong and stuff will break. Right now, few of the self-driving car makers are developing their systems with sufficient redundancy and back-up capabilities. They are so focused on getting a self-driving car to simply drive a car, they figure that once they've got things perfected that then they can go back and look at the resiliency aspects. I understand their logic, but at the same time, trying to bolt onto a system an added layer of redundancy is better done at the start, rather than trying to kludge it later on.

If a camera on the front right bumper goes bad, the AI should detect it. Images might be blurred or otherwise no longer interpretable. The AI needs to then consider what else to do. Assuming that there is a camera up on the hood on the right side, this camera now might need to be considered a "primary" for purposes of detecting things in front of the car on the right side since the camera on the right side bumper is considered out-of-commission. The radar and LIDAR to the right might now become more vital, making up for the failed camera on the front right bumper. For any instance of a sensor that goes bad, the AI needs to assess what else on the self-driving car can potentially make-up for the loss. It is like having someone poke you in one eye, and then you need to become dependent upon the other eye. You might also adjust how you walk and move, since you know that you cannot see out of the eye on that side of your body. The self-driving car might need to do the same, hampering certain kinds of maneuvers that the car would usually make, or even ruling out some maneuvers. Maybe the self-driving car opts to only make left turns and not make any right turns, until the sensor can be replaced.

Consider the circumstances of when a sensor might go bad. If the car is in motion, the nature of the failed sensor could lead directly to a severe result. If you are moving at 80 miles per hour and the LIDAR is your only means of seeing ahead, and if the LIDAR suddenly drops dead, you've now got a speeding missile that in a few seconds could ram into something. I realize that for the levels of self-driving cars that require a human driver be ready to take over that you might argue that the human needs to grab the controls in this instance, but as I have repeatedly exhorted this aspect of dropping the control of the car into the lap of a human driver is fraught with great peril (they won't have time to decide what to do, and even if they decide they still need to take physical control).

And, what about the utopia of the level 5 true self-driving car that has presumably no controls at all for the humans to drive the car? What happens when an essential sensor goes bad and there is no provision for the human to drive, even if they or the AI wanted them to do so? This is more than a scary movie, this is real-life that we are heading towards. Level 5 self-driving cars that once a crucial sensor goes bad will potentially enable a multi-ton vehicle to become a grim reaper itching to kill something or somebody, it's a scary plot for sure.

Suppose the self-driving car is stationary and a crucial sensor goes bad. This might be okay in some cases, assuming that the self-driving car is parked and out of the way of traffic. If instead the self-driving car has come to a halt at a red light, and the sensor suddenly fails, now you have a car blocking traffic. Other traffic might be kind and gently steer around the stopped self-driving car. Or, you might have some other car that drives up and doesn't notice the stopped self-driving car, and rams into it, harming the occupants.

You might also have the case similar to my low tire pressure story, in which you start the self-driving car engine, it runs through internal diagnostics to make sure the sensors are good, and then maybe discovers a key sensor that has gone bad. If you are in a self-driving car that is below a level 5, you presumably could decide to disengage the capability that involves the sensor and then drive the car yourself. This also brings up a larger question about the features of a self-driving car, namely, how much should the human driver be allowed to override or turn-off a self-driving car feature? We are used to being able to decide whether to engage cruise control, and we can readily disengage cruise control whenever we want. Should the same be said of the other more advanced capabilities that will be in our self-driving cars? This is an open question and we are seeing some self-driving car makers ignore the issue, while others are deciding a priori whether to allow this or not (we'll likely be seeing regulation on this).

In this discussion, I've pretended that the self-driving car can actually detect that a sensor has gone bad. But, suppose that a sensor is still functioning, but only intermittently? My low tire pressure story is similar to this intermittent aspect in that the sensors seemed to reboot themselves, though it could readily have reoccurred. The AI needs to be able to ascertain not only if a sensor is failed entirely, but also whether it might be buggy and so then take appropriate action. The AI might try to reboot the particular sensor, or might opt to only collect data when the sensor seems to be functioning correctly.

More insidious is the sensor that does not appear to be faulty and yet really is faulty. Suppose the AI is getting streams of data from the LIDAR and so as far as the AI knows it is working properly. Imagine that every two seconds the LIDAR is integrating noise data into the stream, caused by an anomaly. The images being constructed by the AI might not realize that this bogus data is being slipped into the processing. Sensor fusion takes place and the "bad data" gets mixed into the rest of the data. Ghost images or fake images might be appearing. This might lead the AI to take action such as avoiding an obstacle that is not present. The act of avoiding the obstacle might involve doing a radical maneuver that endangers the occupants of the self-driving car. All of this perhaps being caused by a faulty sensor that was not so obviously faulty that it could easily be detected (there is also the instance of a sensor that has been hacked.

It is time to put serious attention into the redundancy and resiliency of self-driving cars. In my opinion, even a true level 5 self-driving car that does not have redundancy and resiliency is a cheap-trick level 5 car. In one sense, it is a car entirely driven by automation, but it is also a potential death trap waiting to harm or kill humans because it is not prepared to handle internal failings of the car itself. A dashboard display that tells you that something has gone awry is not going to be sufficient when us humans are so dependent upon the AI and the self-driving car to drive the car.

Anyway, the silver lining is that there will be a boon in the marketplace for replacing all those bad sensors once they fail, and a spike in skilled labor that can do the replacements will arise shortly after self-driving cars are sold widely. The you-will-be-out-of-a-job car mechanic of the future should not be overly worried that self-driving cars will put them out of business. Instead, with self-driving cars crammed full of specialized equipment, which will surely falter and fail over time, the job prospects for those mechanics is looking pretty good. Time to get my car mechanics license.

CHAPTER 14

ROADWAY DEBRIS COGNITION FOR SELF-DRIVING CARS

CHAPTER 14

ROADWAY DEBRIS COGNITION
FOR SELF-DRIVING CARS

You are driving along on the open highway and enjoying the scenery. There aren't many other cars around and you have opted to put the pedal to the floor. With the top down on your convertible, you have the wind blowing through your hair and you feel like a million bucks. What could mar this perfect picture of driving on the open roads? Roadway debris. Suppose that you suddenly notice up ahead of you that there is an object laying on the road. Upon first spying the object, you can't quite discern what it is. You can tell that it is in your lane. It seems to be several inches high and a few feet wide. Sitting in the middle of your lane, you are pretty sure that you will need to go around it, rather than trying to roll over it. Looking over your shoulder, you check to see if the lane next to you is available so that you can get out of your current lane.

Nearing the object, you can more clearly discern what it is. It's a blown-out tire. The rubber is torn and distorted, but it clearly is the bulky remnant of a tire. Looks like the type of tire that would be on a SUV, definitely larger than the tire on a regular passenger car, and smaller than a tire on a truck. You steer your convertible into the next lane. Now, you are getting really close to the tire. You zip past it and can see more details of the ripped-up rubber. Your guess is that somehow the busted tire ended-up on the highway and probably other cars or trucks have bashed it time and again, rolling over it and pushing it back-and-forth. You glance in your rearview mirror, hoping that other cars upcoming will realize that the tire is sitting there in the middle of the roadway. At night time, it would be hard to see and likely cars and trucks will continue to run over it. Hopefully no one will get

155

panicked and get into an accident because of the debris.

As a human driver, you undoubtedly see roadway debris quite frequently. In my many years of driving the freeways in Los Angeles, I believe that I've seen most everything that has ever dropped onto the road. Clothing is a popular item, often consisting of shoes or coats. Not sure how people are losing their shoes and coats while otherwise driving on the freeway, but it seems to be a common occurrence. Lots of car parts are often seen. If I had stopped to pick-up every side-view mirror that I've seen on the freeway, I'd have a warehouse full of them. Ladders sometimes are on the freeway, which makes a lot of sense to me. There are tons of contractors that hang ladders on the side or top of their pick-up trucks, and the odds that they have diligently secured the ladder to the vehicle is probably low. I've seen sofas, chairs, and all kinds of furniture on the freeway, usually spilled out from a moving van that was not well packed and secured.

Fortunately, the debris that I've seen has seldom caused an accident in my presence. Listening constantly to the traffic reports on the radio, I know that these debris happenings do often cause accidents. There are other instances of debris getting onto the roadway, such as when a tanker truck overturns and spills something toxic or flammable onto the street. I am going to focus on normal everyday debris. Things that are extraordinary such as dangerous fluids and such that are a further extension of this topic.

We have every right to assume and believe that a self-driving car should be able to handle roadway debris. Currently, the debris handling capabilities of AI self-driving cars is extremely simplistic and not able to contend with anything complicated. Let's walk through the steps involved in dealing with roadway debris and we'll cover how the AI should be coping with this common and potentially deadly malady.

The first step involves having the self-driving car detect that debris exists and should be given due consideration. Using the various sensors on the self-driving car, the AI should be continually ascertaining whether there is any debris up ahead. Similar to how a human does it, the AI will likely get an initial clue that there is debris on the road, but not be quite sure until getting nearer to the object. The further away the detection occurs is good, since it gives the system time to analyze the situation to figure out what to do. Plus, the earlier it is detected the greater usually the number of options about what to do about the debris.

The cameras on the self-driving car will typically provide visual images that can be scanned to try and detect debris on the roadway. Not a sure thing, though, since the cameras might not have a good angle on the item, or the cameras might be blocked by a car ahead or by dirt sitting on the lenses of the camera. Pairing the visual images with radar, the AI system can try to determine if the radar is pinging off the debris and also therefore affirming that there might be something on the road. LIDAR images are also examined. Using all of the sensory capabilities, a sensor fusion occurs and the AI needs to try and pick the needle out of the haystack. A false positive (falsely thinking that there is debris), can occur, in which case this is possibly Okay as long as the self-driving car does not take sudden and risky action based on a false belief. A false negative (falsely concluding that there isn't debris even though there is debris), can be a serious issue since the self-driving car might end-up hitting the debris or otherwise get into serious driving troubles.

Besides trying to detect if the debris exists, there are other crucial parameters to be determined. What is the distance to the debris? Is the debris in the path of the self-driving car? Is the debris in motion or sitting motionless? How high up does the debris extend? How large is the debris? Does it occupy just a portion of the lane or extend across lanes? These and numerous other aspects need to be rapidly assessed. All of these factors play into what to do about the debris. For some of these questions there won't be a complete answer at first. Only once the self-driving car gets closer to the object will these answers become more fully known. Meanwhile, based on probabilities and conjecture, the AI needs to be assessing what to do, even if it does not yet have a perfect understanding of what the debris is and where it is. Just like humans, assessing the situation involves uncertainties and estimations, utilizing imperfect awareness. If the AI system waits until a perfect understanding has been reached, precious time might have evaporated that could have been used to make decisions to act and carry out needed actions.

By determining the distance to the object and knowing the speed of the self-driving car itself, the AI can begin to formulate plans of what to do. Usually, there will already be templates about various circumstances involving debris. In other words, rather than acting as though the AI has never experienced roadway debris, the AI developers will have hopefully gotten the AI system prepared for the debris circumstances. This can also be done via machine learning, whereby prior situations of debris in the roadway have been captured and analyzed, and the AI system makes use of those prior situations to gauge whether the current situation is applicable to prior experience.

Now the self-driving car needs to figure out what action to take. Should the self-driving car slow down and possibly come to a stop in front of the debris? This might be prudent in some cases, while in other cases this might be disastrous. Imagine if there are other cars behind the self-driving car and they are anxious to continue speeding along the road. Having the self-driving car come to a halt in the middle of the freeway could trigger a domino effect of multiple car crashes. With human drivers this happens too, such as the time that I saw a car driven by an older man come to a halt to avoid hitting a stray bumper laying on the road. Other cars behind him were swerving like mad to avoid hitting him. Their swerving caused the other cars to nearly get hit. It was a mess.

Maybe the self-driving car should try to straddle the debris, rolling over it. But this needs to be carefully considered. Suppose the debris hits the underbelly of the car and damages something? Another approach involves avoiding the debris by switching lanes. Sometimes human drivers swerve momentarily out of their lane into the next lane over. This can be dangerous if there are other cars coming along in those lanes. The self-driving car might opt to switch lanes entirely.

All of these options need to be considered and re-assessed continually. A choice made at a distance of a thousand feet away might not be available anymore if the self-driving car has advanced on the debris and is now only 100 feet away. Awareness of the debris should be increasingly available, which also then causes a re-calibration of the danger and options to select from. You might wonder why not just have the self-driving car automatically switch lanes the moment that it detects debris? This is a rather simplistic solution. It could be that the other lanes aren't open to move into. It could be that there is only one lane. It could be that the moving into another lane might not solve the issue if the debris extends across more than one lane. Etc.

Another aspect that needs to be considered is the other traffic involved in the circumstance. The self-driving car has to assume that other cars will potentially react to the debris. A human driver might suddenly swerve into the path of the self-driving car, or otherwise take an action that limits the options available to the self-driving car. In fact, another car might hit the debris, prior to the self-driving car reaching the debris, and shove it over into the path of the self-driving car wherein beforehand perhaps it wasn't in that path. Or, another car might hit the debris and cause it to splinter, sending fragments all along the roadway.

This brings up that another option for the self-driving car involves hitting the debris. Sometimes, options are so limited that the "best" recourse is to just go ahead and strike the debris. This happened to me one day on a blind curve on a mountain. I came around the bend and there was debris sitting on the road. I could not come to a halt as there were other cars behind me that would have rammed into me. I did not see the debris until the last moment because it was sitting at the corner of the blind curve. I could not have swerved into the oncoming lane of traffic because I would have produced a head-on collision. I ran right into the debris, and prayed that it would not destroy my car and nor harm anyone else. Turns out that it busted part of my bumper and my front turn indicator. At least no one got hurt and I had ended-up pushing it off the road.

What would a self-driving car have done? We need to make sure that self-driving cars have the appropriate smarts to make these kinds of life-and-death decisions. I've focused on a single piece of debris. That's the easy example. Suppose there are multiple pieces of debris, and essentially the road is like an obstacle course, or maybe you might think of it as a minefield. One time, I was driving along, minding my own business, when all of a sudden a truck ahead of me dropped a half dozen cans of white paint onto the freeway. I rolled over the cans, but they had already punctured and there was white paint splashing all about. I carefully exited from the freeway to see what might have happened to the underbelly of my car. When I stopped at a gas station, I laid on the ground to look under the car. I was now the proud owner of a car that had white paint splashed all over the underbelly of the car. Fortunately, it did not seem to have caused any harm. I was also lucky that the white paint could not be seen while standing and looking at the car (my car was all black in color, the white would have shown easily).

Roadway debris is a common occurrence and AI self-driving cars need to have the cognitive capabilities involved in ascertaining what to do about debris. A one-size-fits-all approach of for example always hitting debris or always avoiding debris is not very sound. There are circumstances where hitting the debris is prudent, while in other cases hitting it would be a terrible choice. Likewise, there are circumstances that dictate avoiding the debris is the best option. Whichever it is, we are going to rely on our self-driving cars to figure this out. For those self-driving cars that are less than the topmost Level 5, some car makers are assuming that the human driver will figure out what needs to be done. As I have repeated stated, the notion of suddenly handing control back to the human and have them make a split-second decision is risky and outright dangerous. AI developers and the auto makers need to ensure that self-driving cars have roadway debris acumen. I am looking for my self-driving car to be roadway savvy, and so should you.

CHAPTER 15

AVOIDING PEDESTRIAN ROADKILL BY SELF-DRIVING CARS

CHAPTER 15

AVOIDING PEDESTRIAN ROADKILL BY SELF-DRIVING CARS

A reporter for a major news publication was recently invited to take a ride in one of the prominent so-called self-driving cars (I question whether we can reasonably call today's automation-enhanced cars as self-driving, see my piece on this question). Eagerly accepting the offer, the reporter chronicled the trip and even recorded video that was then posted with the reported story. In the video, the car approached an intersection and though the car had the right-of-way, it came to a crawl when it spotted a pedestrian that had made a motion at the far edge of the pedestrian walkway as though the person was going to enter into the crosswalk. The reporter commented on the timid nature of the automation that was driving the car. A human driver would have likely barreled ahead, unless perhaps the human driver was someone just learning to drive. We've all seen those neophyte drivers in the marked vehicles that warn you they are a student driver and you should be on the ready for them to hit the brakes or make some other overly cautious maneuver.

Being exceedingly cautious in driving a car is generally a good practice, but of course not if it tends to confound other drivers and inadvertently lead to a collision. The reporter was probably lucky that a car behind the self-driving car did not slam into them. Other drivers that would have perceived the pedestrian as not a threat would be frustrated by the sudden slow down and might have been caught unawares that the self-driving car wanted to suddenly slow down. There is a delicate dance of cars and pedestrians. Cars react to pedestrians. Pedestrians react to cars. Furthermore, there can be a domino or cascading effect too. A car might react to a pedestrian, which then causes other cars to react to both the pedestrian and the reaction of the first car that exhibited a reaction. Or, we might have a pedestrian that reacts to a car, and then suddenly have other pedestrians all reacting too. There are lots of combinations and permutations in the dance of the pedestrians and cars.

In the self-driving car arena, one of the more famous examples of a self-driving car reaction to a pedestrian involved an Uber self-driving car in San Francisco. The Uber self-driving car essentially skyrocketed through a red light at an intersection, meanwhile there was a pedestrian in the crosswalk, though admittedly the pedestrian was far from danger of actually getting hit by the self-driving car. I suppose we've all done this kind of thing before, wherein we rush a yellow light that went to red as we zoomed past a pedestrian standing in the crosswalk (well, I'm not saying I've ever done this, just to be clear). The act of the Uber car was caught on video and posted for all the world to witness. Uber then pulled their self-driving cars out of California temporarily due to the bad press that they got on this incident. As I've mentioned in my other pieces, Uber just happened to get caught on video and I assure you that the other self-driving cars have all done the same kind of action at one time or another.

Let's do a quick recap. I've described an incident by one self-driving car that came to a crawl because it spotted a pedestrian, while we have another incident of a self-driving car that presumably did not spot the pedestrian and unknowingly zipped along. Woe is the pedestrian. Today's self-driving cars are still trying to figure out the nature of pedestrians and what to do about them. You might be surprised to know that dealing with pedestrians is actually a rather difficult problem for self-driving cars. Human drivers after a while become accustomed to the vagaries of pedestrians and develop various rules-of-the-road and intuition about what pedestrians are going to do. Plus, since human drivers have themselves been or are pedestrians at times, they have learned what cars driven by other humans will do in reacting to pedestrians.

If you've ever been to New York City (NYC), you might have witnessed the delicate and at times crass dance of the pedestrians and the cars that seems to take place in that particular cultural milieu. Generally, pedestrians in New York City do not seem to believe that they need to abide by the laws involving the proper ways to cross a street. Jaywalking is considered to be a right. Often, the NYC pedestrian will give a glaring stare at a human driver, as though the jaywalker is telegraphing don't tread on me, and so the car driver backs down to let the pedestrian cross. Some NYC human drivers though also provide a hardened stare in return, as though they are daring the pedestrian to cross the street. All of this is somewhat akin to running with the bulls at Pamplona. This is a kind of dance that can lead to someone getting gored.

In other cities like Boston and Los Angeles, the stare-down can be completely different. Bostonians seem to prefer to not stare at each other, trying to pretend that neither of them exist. If there is eye contact made between pedestrian and driver then something has to be decided between them. On the other hand, by just stepping off the sidewalk and walking into the street without making eye contact, the Bostonian pedestrian is saying that they have the right-of-way. You would almost think this could lead to greater calamity than the NYC approach, but for locals it seems to do okay. In Los Angeles, there tends to be a politer kind of stare-down, involving one stare saying go ahead and another kind of stare saying don't you dare make the first move.

Why is this pertinent to self-driving cars? Right now, self-driving cars don't do anything about trying to communicate with pedestrians. In fact, it is an incredible technological feat for a self-driving car to even identify that a pedestrian exists, let alone try to predict the behavior of the pedestrian and get into their mind. Gradually, we will ultimately have self-driving cars that can understand "the theory of mind" involving pedestrians and even other drivers, but we are a long way from that day.

I realize that some of you might be yelling out that there are pedestrian detection capabilities on today's cars and asking what about those capabilities. Owners of certain Toyota model cars are perhaps already familiar with the pedestrian detection that Toyota provides. Known as PCS with PD (that's code for Pre-Collision System with Pedestrian Detection), the car is equipped with a camera aimed forward of the car and also with a front-grill mounted radar device. The radar and the camera try to work together and figure out whether a pedestrian is in-front of the car. If a pedestrian is detected, or believed to have been detected, the automation assists the human driver of the car. An audio and visual alert tries to warn the human driver to take cautionary or evasive action. A human driver that responds by braking will then get added assistance by the automation, which can apply even greater force to the braking, in an effort to aid the human driver. In certain circumstances, if the human driver does not react and try to brake, then the PCS/PD of the car will automatically start applying the brakes in an effort to avoid striking the pedestrian.

Though the PCS with PD should be applauded for what it tries to do, let's be forthright and acknowledge that this is barely any true sense of pedestrian detection. The limitations of this existing technology are huge. First, it will only spot pedestrians that are directly in front of the car. Pedestrians coming at your car from the side are not going to be readily detected. When going in reverse, pedestrians behind you are not going to be detected. Toyota freely concedes that pedestrians might not be detected at all, depending upon their size, their profile, their motion, their angle to the car, the brightness of the lighting around the car, etc.

For developers of self-driving car automation, you might want to take a look at OpenCV. This is a large-scale open source effort toward creating sophisticated Computer Vision (CV) capabilities. OpenCV has been used for pedestrian detection and provides some fascinating insights about how hard a problem this is. The simplest example of detecting a pedestrian involves looking at a picture and trying to find the pedestrian in that picture. At first, most of the pedestrian detection algorithms could not differentiate between say a telephone pole and a human. They were both vertical in height and so might be considered alike. These algorithms were modified to find the vertical height as a torso and then also look for a head, arms, and legs. This reduces the number of the false positives, such as no longer categorizing a telephone pole or other such objects as pedestrians. In essence, it went from looking for a blob to looking for a structure with certain characteristics.

There are though other false positives that can readily pass the test of looking for these human physical characteristics. For example, a road sign that shows a stick figure of a person can be misconstrued as an actual human pedestrian because the cartoon drawing has a torso, arms, legs, and a head. Similarly, a bronze statue of a mayor that might be at a corner or on the sidewalk near to the roadway could be misconstrued as a pedestrian. In one sense, it is usually safer to mistakenly identify a false positive than it does to make the mistake of generating a false negative. A false negative occurs when the pedestrian detection fails to detect that a pedestrian might be present.

Why would automation fail to detect a pedestrian? There are currently numerous ways that a pedestrian will not be "seen" by automation. Using a camera alone is extremely weak as a detection method because the picture might be unable to showcase that a pedestrian exists in the photo. Imagine a photo taken in bright sunlight with the photo all washed out due to the brightness of the sun. The pedestrian might be in the photo but the overly white area of the picture causes them to not be readily detected. Even if the photo is pristine, suppose the pedestrian is standing perfectly still and has their arms pressed to their body and their legs are tightly touching. Remember when you were a child and tried to hide by compressing your body? This can happen by chance, and it makes detection harder because the photo analysis might not reveal that there are arms and legs, which is considered a clue to whether the pedestrian is there or not.

There might also be occlusion in the photo, involving one object hiding another object. I was standing at an intersection the other day when a Fedex worker with a dolly had a big box that he was hoping to deliver across the street. From the perspective of a human driver in the roadway, all you would have seen was a large box and barely even his head, which was slightly sticking up above the box. Whenever objects are in front of a pedestrian, such as the box and the Fedex worker, it will make photo detection of the pedestrian much harder. You can even have multiple pedestrians all standing together, and it will be hard to differentiate between one pedestrian and the other pedestrians. One particularly notable danger in a group setting is the classic case of a small child that suddenly darts out from a crowd of pedestrians.

Keep in mind that pedestrians come in all shapes and sizes. There are small children to be detected. There are elderly to be detected. There are individuals to be detected. There are groups of pedestrians to be detected. Is that a parent holding the hand of a child? Is that a blind person with a cane? These are all the kinds of pedestrian detection that we as human drivers do on a daily basis. If you ask a student driver whether or not they saw a pedestrian standing on the sidewalk, they often cannot tell you for sure whether they saw the pedestrian. The student driver is so consumed with driving the car that they had not yet perfected the ability to also look for pedestrians. Self-driving cars are in that same boat today.

Notice that I have been discussing the detection of pedestrians in photos. Let's up the ante. We know that pedestrians aren't always going to be standing still and happily smiling to have their picture taken. The real trick involves video analysis for pedestrians. A true pedestrian detection system needs to find pedestrians within moving images. The OpenCV effort provides examples of how hard it is to gauge pedestrians while they are in motion. One moment the pedestrian might be easily detected, and the next moment as they walk behind an electrical junction box they are occluded and disappear from view. Trying to find pedestrians when they are in motion can be very tricky.

Making the pedestrian detection doubly tricky, you need to also realize that the car itself will also likely be in motion. Sure, there are cases when the car is waiting at an intersection and is motionless due to a red light or a stop sign, but most of the time the car will be zooming along. You therefore have a car in motion that is trying to capture video of humans that are in motion. The blur effect can be tremendous. You've probably taken pictures from a moving car and gotten a blurred image of what is around you. The automation needs to try and overcome the blur and figure out what's actually in the pictures or video.

Plus, all of this pedestrian detection needs to be done in real-time. It's one thing to have a photo or video that you can run computer programs to analyze and let the analysis take hours to do, but it is another game entirely to have to find pedestrians in real-time and within split seconds be able to discern what is a pedestrian and what is not. A car moving along on the road at 20 miles per hour is taking in streams of video and must be continually analyzing it to find the pedestrians. This takes tremendous processing power and lots of computing to do. Self-driving cars are gradually getting loaded with lots of computing to handle these kinds of tasks, and the increasing miniaturization of computer processors and their decreasing costs are an important contributor toward advances in self-driving cars.

So far, I've focused mainly on pedestrian detection in this discussion. Yes, knowing that a pedestrian exists is crucial to dealing with pedestrians, but it is only the start. You need to also figure out what the pedestrian is going to do. If a pedestrian has already appeared in front of your car, let's say they have been standing in the middle of the road, it is pretty easy to decide that maybe the car should take some evasive action. On the other hand, if the pedestrian is innocently standing to the side of the road, you need to have some kind of smarts to predict what the pedestrian is going to do next. Is it the type of person that is more or less likely to suddenly run into the road? This is where predictive capabilities and the theory of mind comes to play.

I was driving down the street in a residential neighborhood one day, minding my own business, and I happened to see out of the corner of my eye a teenage boy crouching over near some bushes up ahead. I didn't think much about this aspect since he was quite a distance from the roadway. All of a sudden, he stood-up, his arm raised and he hurled something. It happened very fast and I could not see what he was tossing. To my shock and surprise, my windshield suddenly became all blurred and I could barely look out the car. He had tossed a water balloon at my windshield and the exploding balloon dispersed a wave of water across the glass. Within a split second or two, I realized it was water and hastily turned on my windshield wipers. This had been a very dangerous act by the teenager since I could have swerved off the road, or maybe have hit a pedestrian that might have been in front of my car but that I couldn't see due to the sudden water occlusion on my windshield.

Would a self-driving car and its pedestrian detection be able to predict that the teenage boy might toss something at the car? Maybe yes, maybe no. With the advent of machine learning, and with self-driving cars that share their learning with each other, if one such self-driving car had this same encounter it would share it with the other cars so they too would be on the watch for this. In my own personal case, I now seem to be especially wary whenever I see someone crouching off the side of the road. Don't want to seem paranoid and I realize the odds of this happening again is slim. The point simply is that once experienced, it is a scenario that can become part of one's experience, and also be generalized to cover other like situations that might occur.

I had mentioned earlier that in various cities there is a cultural basis for the dance between the pedestrian and cars. If self-driving cars are made to overly flinch when it detects a pedestrian, as happened to the reporter that I mentioned at the start of today's piece, pedestrians are sure to figure this out. In other words, pedestrians tend to adopt to the behaviors of the drivers. If I know that I can fake out a self-driving car and get it to slow down or stop, merely by making a head-fake toward the road, I am probably going to do so, either for fun or because I want to cross the road and make sure the car allows me to do so. I am predicting that for each of the models and brands of self-driving cars, they will each have their own tolerances of pedestrian detection and reaction, and eventually pedestrians will know which such cars to challenge and which to acquiesce to.

The pedestrian detection will get better as more sensory devices are added into the mix of the self-driving cars. I mentioned that the Toyota cars are using both cameras and a radar device. This combination is handy. If the camera provides images that are blurred or unable to be readily analyzed, the radar provides a secondary way to detect pedestrians. If the radar has troubles getting a detection, then the camera provides a back-up method for it. By having several sensory devices and doing a proper job of sensor fusion, the odds of getting true detections is increased, and the odds of false positives and false negatives goes down.

One of the claimed advantages of self-driving cars is that they will eliminate all pedestrian injuries or deaths due to colliding with cars. I have debunked this notion in one of my pieces. It will be quite a while before we'll have self-driving cars that can be as appropriately wary of pedestrians as savvy humans are. The self-driving car makers are slowly gaining ground into the pedestrian detection realm, mainly right now with only simplistic methods. I expect that we will soon have a self-driving car crisis-in-faith because some self-driving car will plow into a pedestrian. It is bound to happen. Let's try to get the self-driving car makers to avoid this calamity and put more effort into their pedestrian detection and reaction systems. I vote for no roadkill's.

CHAPTER 16

WHEN ACCIDENTS HAPPEN TO SELF-DRIVING CARS

Lance B. Eliot

CHAPTER 16

WHEN ACCIDENTS HAPPEN
TO SELF-DRIVING CARS

Sinkholes. We recently had a major sinkhole that opened up in the middle of a busy street here in Southern California, and it swallowed whole the two cars that happened to unluckily be driving along the street at that time. Imagine being able to tell your friends that your car fell into a sinkhole. Your car didn't hit a pothole, it didn't sideswipe a telephone pole, it didn't get hit by lightning, instead it fell into a sinkhole. That's some great bragging rights.

One of the cars that had fallen into the sinkhole had only sank a brief distance and was caught on top of the first car that fell into the hole. The back portion of this second car protruded out of the sinkhole, raising up a few feet above street level. The woman driver in the car was able to get out, partially aided by the fire department which had shown up to rescue the people in both vehicles. She was slightly injured, but otherwise Okay from the ordeal. I suspect though that she is going to be envisioning the street opening up whenever she drives around town from now on. Anyway, her car was still in gear when she managed to extradite herself from the vehicle. On the newscast of the event, the rear tires of the car were shown spinning vigorously as the vehicle thought it was still trying to drive along the street. This actually made for a dangerous situation since no one knew what the now abandoned car might do next. Gradually, it lurched forward and sank deeper into the sinkhole and eventually stopped running.

Why my fascination with cars that got swallowed by the earth? The one car that had kept running is an example of what a car might do when in an accident. In other words, some car accidents involve a car crash that causes the car to stop functioning. Other accidents might involve a car that still has the engine running, which can create a grave hazard for everyone near the scene of the accident. It has been the case that some cars in a car crash have suddenly moved forward or backward, endangering the driver, passengers, and rescuers. There is also a heightened chance of a fire or maybe even an explosion, since the car is engaged and there is fuel flowing to the engine, along with likely sparks and hot pieces of metal around the accident scene. All in all, a car accident and the surrounding scene can be a very dangerous place.

Let's consider what will happen when self-driving cars are involved in an accident. Now, some of the ardent proponents of self-driving cars will immediately counter that there is no such thing as a self-driving car getting into accident. They are of the camp that believes that self-driving cars will be an idealized world wherein no cars will ever get into accidents again. This is plain hogwash. I have repeatedly stated there are falsehoods about zero fatalities related to self-driving cars and that there will still be car accidents, in spite of whatever wondrous AI we see embodied into self-driving cars. There are going to be a mix of human driven cars and self-driving cars for quite a while, and the two are bound to tango with each other. There are also lots of other opportunities for self-driving cars to get into accidents, including if the self-driving car has a severe hardware failure within itself, and also if the AI of the self-driving car encounters a bug in the software, and so on.

Assume for now that it is quite possible and actually very probable that self-driving cars will get into accidents. So what, you ask? The issue is that if the AI system of the self-driving car is still active, what will it do? For a human driver in a car accident, the human usually opts to stop trying to drive the car. They typically will try to get out of the damaged car and step away from the mechanical beast. This is not always the case, and of course if the car accident is minor, the human driver might decide to drive off from the scene. We also know about circumstances of hit-and-run, wherein the human driver hits someone or something, and tries to scoot away without anyone else knowing what happened.

An AI-based self-driving car will need to be self-aware enough to know that the car has gotten into an accident. Humans know this pretty quickly by having felt the blow of the accident, they can see the crushed metal and blood, they are physically hurt or restrained, they can smell burnt metal or spilled gasoline, and so on. There are lots of physical sensory clues for humans. A disembodied AI computer-based system won't necessarily be able to gauge these same physical clues. Sure, the car will likely have come to a sudden halt, which is a clue that something is amiss. The cameras on the car might have seen the accident and the AI system can interpret the images captured accordingly. We could have other sensors in the car such as impact sensors and other devices that realize the car has gotten itself into trouble.

The key is then whether the AI system of the self-driving car knows what to do, once it detects that a car accident has indeed happened. The AI system might continue to try driving the car, pushing on the accelerator, even though the car no longer can or should be driving. It is like the example I gave before of the car that fell into the sinkhole and the tires continued to spin. That was a "dumb" car that did not have any AI smarts. AI developers for self-driving cars need to make sure that the system can detect that an accident has happened, and then take appropriate actions based on the accident. This might include applying the brakes, turning off the engine, and taking other safety precautions.

Will though the AI self-driving car still be able to process information and take actions? Remember that once the accident has occurred, all bets are off as to what parts of the car are still functioning. Maybe the AI system no longer has access to any of the controls of the car. Or, maybe the AI system itself is being powered by the car, but now the car is no longer running and the battery was ejected from the car during the accident. No power, no AI. All of these variations mean that we don't know for sure that the self-driving car will be in a shape needed to take the appropriate safety precautions.

It is also possible that part of the AI system itself is damaged during the accident. Some sensors might be entirely offline. Some sensors might be working, but are noisy and incomplete. Some sensors might be "working" but providing incorrect data because they are no longer functioning as intended. Imagine if a sensor that detects the motion of the car is damaged in such a manner that it falsely reports that the car is still driving forward. The AI, if functioning, might be misled into trying to command the controls of the car in an untoward manner. Any passengers or rescuers could be put into danger because of these facets.

Some believe that fire departments and police should have an electronic backdoor into the AI system of the car, so that upon coming upon a self-driving car accident scene, the humans can communicate directly with the AI system. They can use this communication link to instruct the self-driving car to do things, such as turn off the engine of the car. They can use the link to find out what happened in the car accident. The AI might also know how many passengers there are in the car. This could help the rescue efforts, since the responders would know how many people to be rescued. For many important reasons, this backdoor electronic communication makes a lot of sense.

As with any of these aspects, there are downsides to an electronic backdoor. Will only the proper officials use the backdoor, or could a nefarious hacker use it to take over the controls of your car? Even if the backdoor is there, maybe the AI system is so damaged that any information it provides is incorrect or misleading. One might also wonder about the privacy aspects of this electronic backdoor too. Will humans be comfortable that anything the AI system has recorded could now so easily be scanned by someone else, doing so without a legal search warrant?

Self-driving car makers are considering having the same kind of black boxes in their self-driving cars as are found in modern airplanes. This black-box hardened casing of crucial systems would not only record information, but also try to protect the AI system so that it could continue to function in an accident. This might not be the entire AI system, and perhaps just a core portion that can do fundamental activities and no more.

There are also advanced efforts to make AI systems more resilient so that if only part of the AI system is still functioning, the other parts recognize as such, and then adjust accordingly. For example, suppose the AI system portion that provides the steering and mapping gets damaged, other parts of the AI system can either try to operate those aspects as a secondary back-up, or take into account that those functions are no longer working and avoid anything that requires those functions. This adds a lot of complexity to the AI system, but given that the self-driving car involves the life-and-death matters of humans, having sufficient complexity to protect humans is worth the added effort.

The AI system can even have a component devoted to saving humans when the car gets into a crash. Suppose the AI system is able to release the seat belts, automatically, when it so chooses to do so. Once a car crash has occurred, passengers might be trapped in the car and unable to reach their seatbelt releases. Or, the passengers might be unconscious. The AI system, assuming it is working properly during the crash aftermath, could take actions that would help the passengers and aid rescuers. This comes with the downside that the AI system might make the wrong choice, like release a seatbelt that was holding a human that was upside down in a rolled over car, and they then drop to floor and get hurt by the seemingly innocent and helpful act intended by the AI system.

Few of the self-driving car makers are putting much attention to what the AI system should do during an accident. They are blissfully unaware of the considerations. They figure that once the car crashes, the AI system is no longer involved in what happens next. There could be some kind of switch that tries to automatically disengage the AI once the car crashes, and so it turns the car into one large somewhat immovable multi-ton object. This can be useful in some crashes, and not so useful in others. For example, suppose the car crash left the car still drivable, and you wanted to get the car off the road and onto a side street. In what instances should the AI be auto-disconnected and in other cases left on to help get the car out of the way or to greater safety?

AI researchers are looking at machine learning as an aid for figuring out what to do during a car crash. Imagine if you had the "experience" of thousands and thousands of car crashes and so could try to discern what to do during any particular car crash. This can especially be crucial when the moment of the car crash begins, since the evasive actions of the self-driving car can potentially produce fewer deaths and injuries. The self-driving car might realize that swerving will lessen the impact to the passengers, or maybe sharply hitting the brakes might reduce the injuries. This also raises the question of the ethics of the AI.

I am keenly of the camp that says let's not leave to chance what will happen when a self-driving car gets into an accident. We need to be explicit about what the car and AI will do. We need to know whether there are redundancies and safeguards built into the AI system and the overall systems of the self-driving car. If we don't carefully think about this, it will be by "accident" that when accidents happen that people are saved or killed. I would rather that my self-driving car has a purposeful built-in approach to handling accidents. We know for sure that self-driving cars aren't going to be accident free, and so car makers need to make the cars as smart to drive as they are smart enough to cope with accidents.

CHAPTER 17
ILLEGAL DRIVING FOR
SELF-DRIVING CARS

CHAPTER 17

ILLEGAL DRIVING FOR
SELF-DRIVING CARS

Here in California, we have carpool lanes, which are also known as diamond lanes (marked with a diamond symbol), and officially called High-Occupancy Vehicle (HOV) lanes.

These special lanes are intended to alleviate traffic congestion by encouraging two or more occupiers in a car. This helps to maximize the people-carrying capacity of our roadways. If you've been to Southern California during a recent visit, you've likely experienced the non-stop bumper-to-bumper freeway traffic that we seem to have year-round now, in spite of also having these HOV lanes. It can be maddening and exasperating to drive across town and take two hours to go a mere 20 miles in distance.

One interesting aspect of the carpool lanes involves their design. Most of the carpool lanes are at the leftmost positional lane of the freeway, generally where you would normally expect a so-called fast lane to be. The carpool lanes used to be wide open such that any car could wander into and out of the carpool lane, doing so at any juncture. Studies showed that this was actually making traffic worse and leading to a heightened volume of car accidents, and that a controlled entry point and exit point for the use of carpool lanes made more sense. Drivers were wildly entering and exiting from the carpool lanes, ramming into each other and often moving from a fast rate of speed into the lane next to it that was proceeding at a much slower clip or faster clip. Imagine going 70 mph and suddenly merging to your right into a lane moving at 15 mph. It was a recipe for disaster.

The cost to potentially erect physical barriers along miles and miles of carpool lanes was quite high, and so instead the idea of painting double-yellow lines onto the freeway surface was used (indicative of do not cross it), and was coupled with occasional dashed or broken white lines (meaning Okay to cross). Thus, in California, it is against the law to cross a solid double-yellow line, therefore for that portion of the carpool lane that has the solid double-yellow line you cannot legally enter into or exit from the carpool lane. You must only enter or exit whenever there is a broken white line. These broken or dashed white lines painted onto the freeway are staggered here and there, allowing exit or entry every few miles or whenever the thought was that drivers might be needing to get out to say reach the Disneyland exit or some other popular freeway exit or entrance.

As you can guess, not everyone is willing to abide by these painted lines. Legal scofflaws will often jump into and out of the carpool lane, arbitrarily crossing that solid double-yellow line, trying to quicken their way to work or get to that happy hour bar they are aiming for after work. Crossing the carpool lanes illegally is generally a violation of the California driving code CVC 21655.8 and if you are caught doing so then you are likely to have to pay a hefty fine of several hundred dollars and be given a point on your driving record by the Department of Motor Vehicles (DMV) denoting that you incurred a moving violation (as you accumulate points you endanger losing your privilege to drive on California public roads).

It is clearly stated in California that it is illegal to cross the solid double-yellow lines of a carpool lane. I am a very law abiding citizen and always obey the rules of the carpool lane. I angrily glare at those that illegally use the carpool lanes and I anxiously look around in hopes that a highway patrol officer might pull them over. Besides giving them a ticket, I somehow also dreamily hope that maybe they might get a bit roughed up too. I say this in jest, of course, but I do think that these drivers are creating undue risk for all of us on the freeways and that it is not just that they themselves are taking risks, but that they are also putting all the rest of us at higher risk too. They are inconsiderate and selfish, and so whatever punishment can be applied is good with me. Dare I say, the death penalty?

The other day, I was driving along, solo, and cruising along in the regular lanes of traffic. Up ahead, two cars had bashed into each other and were sitting in the middle of the freeway. No first responders had yet arrived and this was a freshly minted car accident. The cars behind this traffic roadblock were trying to flow around the blockage, akin to a stream of water trying to flow around a large boulder sitting in the middle of the river. I was going to need to choose whether to flow to the left of the wreck, or flow to the right of the wreck. The right side was full of cars all now being squeezed into one lane of space, and it was pure pandemonium of drivers jockeying for position. Flowing to the left would have been much easier. The catch was that on the left side was the carpool lane, and at a juncture of the solid double-yellow lines.

Yes, cars were now illegally going into the carpool lane, including I am betting many drivers that would never think of violating the golden rule of don't cross the carpool lane when it is a solid double-yellow. They were all subject to getting tickets. There was no question that they were violating the legal rule.

Why have I dragged you through the somewhat arcane aspects of carpool lanes in California? The reason is that I want to bring up an important topic about self-driving cars and AI. For some proponents of self-driving cars, they rave about the aspect that the beauty of self-driving cars is that they won't drive illegally. All those crazy human drivers that violate the rules of the road will someday be in a self-driving car that will presumably obey all traffic laws. The idea of traffic tickets will disappear. We won't even remember the time during which there was a need to have traffic cops and issue traffic tickets. The court system will dispense with the traffic courts and we'll all live a happy ticket-free life. What a wonderful future!

But, I say that this utopian view is out of touch with reality. Let's take a look at why this concept of ticket-free and always lawful self-driving cars is a rather simplistic and frankly ill-informed idea.
I'd like to revisit the carpool lane circumstance that I just described. The cars were flowing around the accident scene and some of the cars went into the carpool lane illegally to do so. Were they wrong to flow into the carpool lane?

Well, it depends upon your perspective. There is a "necessity defense" that one can use in court to claim that an illegal driving act was necessary due to roadway conditions. For example, someone has their wife in their car and she is pregnant and about to deliver her baby, so the husband drives above the posted speed limit to get to the hospital in time. The driver broke the law by driving above the posted speed limit. A judge can toss out the ticket if it is believed that the driver violated the law for a bona fide reason and did so with sufficient care and lack of recklessness. This is pretty much a case-to-case type of defense, though prior precedent comes to play too.

If you are in a self-driving car, what will the AI do in these kinds of circumstances? Some want the AI system to rigorously and always obey the law. Period. No exceptions. This is certainly the easier way to write the AI system. By avoiding having to consider anything other than the stated rules of the road, it is much easier to program the system. Basically, input the entire driving manual and rules of the locale you are in, and as an AI programmer you can call it a day. This though seems lacking in realism and ultimately people are going to be upset that their self-driving car is a "mindless robot" that cannot discern when to consider exceptions to the rules.

Consider the case of the cars flowing around the freeway snarl. Would your self-driving car be willing to flow into the carpool lane, crossing the solid double-yellow lines? If programmed to strictly obey the law, it would not do so. It would either sit on the freeway and remain standing behind the traffic snarl and wait for the wreckage to be cleared, or might veer to the right side of the wreckage. But, suppose the right side consisted of an area that was actually not a lane and was the edge of the roadway.

Suppose further that it was illegal to drive on that far edge. Now what? Again, would the self-driving car opt to just sit on the freeway and wait to see what happens? Suppose that the freeway is occupied by only self-driving cars and no human driven cars, then this would bring the entire freeway to a potential cascading halt. It could be a domino effect that leads to miles and miles of road stoppage, all because the "mindless" self-driving cars are strictly abiding by the law.

Some will counterargue that this kind of predicament is rare and only occurs once in a blue moon. I disagree. I vehemently disagree. This is not an alleged "edge problem" (which programmers consider a rare circumstance in requirements and thus can be generally ignored or shuffled into a let's get to it later on bin). This idea of being flexible regarding the laws is actually very common. It happens every day and by millions of drivers everywhere. Thinking of this as a rarity is like looking at driving through rose colored glasses. Driving is messy. It is not like a video game or some idealized world.

If you buy into my claim that self-driving cars will need to be willing to drive illegally, the next aspect is when and under what conditions will they do so. We don't want the AI to just do so whenever it darned well pleases. We need to still enforce the laws so as to ensure that by-and-large we don't end-up with chaos and carnage on the roads. The AI needs to consider the options available when driving, including gauging whether an illegal act is warranted.

Ultimately, the AI system will be responsible, or someone that made it will be responsible, or maybe we might even decide that the passengers are responsible (though this has great controversy associated with it). At some point, the choices made to drive illegally by an AI-based self-driving car will need to be reviewed and ascertained as to whether it was a good choice or not.

Being ultra-futuristic, you could suggest that maybe the self-driving car AI system could ask a special AI-based real-time tribunal whether the self-driving car can make an illegal driving move in a particular instance, and so in real-time get pre-approved to take such an act. Again, this is a somewhat utopian view and unlikely to be enacted within any reasonably foreseeable future right now. You could also suggest that due to machine learning, and if self-driving cars are sharing their experiences, the impetus to take one illegal act could be based on having "learned" about other times that self-driving cars performed an illegal act. This though is fraught with other difficulties, including whether the situation that your self-driving car currently faces is truly akin to whatever was "learned" via machine learning. If the facts of your situation differ, even in a small way, the learned response from others might not be valid and your self-driving car could make a bad choice because of it.

Consider too the consequences associated with a self-driving car making illegal driving moves. One possible consequence is that the self-driving car maybe will create an accident and cause harm by performing the illegal act. If the self-driving car opts to go into the carpool lane illegally, as described by my example earlier about the freeway blockage, and suppose that it does so without realizing that a car that was legally in the carpool lane cannot slowdown in time and hits the self-driving car, this obviously can produce a bad result. Remember too that we are not discussing a world of all self-driving cars, in that for the foreseeable future we are going to have a mixture of human driven cars and self-driving cars. I say this because if the world had only self-driving cars, in theory they could communicate with each other and try to coordinate their activities. Thus, the self-driving car trying to barge into the carpool lane could have told the approaching self-driving car that is legally in the carpool lane to slow down and let in the illegally acting self-driving car.

I'll end this discussion with some added twists to this illegal driving of self-driving cars diatribe. The other day I drove up to an intersection that was controlled by a traffic signal. The light was red to me. I came to a full stop, behind the pedestrian walkway for crossing the intersection. A man in a bright orange vest began to walk through the intersection and he was pushing a rolling device that was painting the pedestrian lines. He got about halfway through the intersection, and then realized he could not complete his effort in the time allotted for the red light. He then held up his hand for me and the other cars that were waiting for the green light. We all took this to mean that we should please wait until he had finished his task.

Sure enough, our light went green, and not a single car moved forward. I was impressed at how his use of his hand had magically gotten all of us to disobey the green light. Cars further behind us were likely confused about why we weren't moving. I fully expected to hear some horns honking. It was also a bit dangerous too, since cars coming from behind us could see the green light, and might inadvertently plow into the back of our cars.

You need to ask yourself this question: What would a self-driving car do?

The light was clearly green. The self-driving car, if merely "taught" to work legally, would assume it can proceed since the light is green. Even if it knew not to hit the worker that was painting the street, he was now over to the side, and so the self-driving car could have proceeded without harming the worker. But, this also would not have been with the realization that the worker wanted to make his way back across the path, due to his wanting to make two coats of paint on the street surface. Can we expect our self-driving cars to be able to figure out this kind of driving complexity? It would need to have understood the gesture by the worker, it would have needed to understand the aspects of what the worker was doing, it would have had to understand the meaning of the green light and when to go and not, etc.

This is why the true self-driving cars, the Level 5, which is a self-driving car that is driven entirely by the AI and does not need any human driving intervention, those Level 5 cars are a lot harder to achieve than you might at first glance believe. We'll need to make sure that the self-driving cars know when to drive illegally, and that illegal driving is an option. It cannot be a fait accompli that self-driving cars will always and only drive legally. They need to be that maverick sometimes. But hopefully in a way that causes good and not harm. I'll want to be there the day that the true Level 5 self-driving car gets its first ticket and its first point against its driving privileges, and then argues that the illegal act was a necessity and gets the ticket tossed and the point removed. That's the day that the illegally driving self-driving car has grown-up

CHAPTER 18

MAKING SENSE OF

ROAD SIGNS

FOR SELF-DRIVING CARS

Lance B. Eliot

CHAPTER 18

MAKING SENSE OF ROAD SIGNS FOR SELF-DRIVING CARS

Road signs.

Can't live with them, can't live without them.

A few years ago, I was tricked (I claim) by a road sign that was being used by a motorcycle cop to write numerous traffic tickets. Here's my story. In downtown Los Angeles, there is a popular one-way street that reaches another popular one-way street that is perpendicular to it. Everybody comes up to the corner to make a right turn from one of those streets onto the other. When there is a red light, of course traffic normally comes to a full stop prior to trying to make the right turn, and proceeds only when the pedestrian walkway is empty and otherwise it is legal to proceed. This particular right turn is well known and frequented by especially the evening heading-home-from-work downtown drivers.

So, having made that same turn hundreds of times, I drive up to it one evening around 6 p.m., I dutifully came to a full stop since the traffic light was red, I made sure there was no one in the pedestrian walkway, and then I made the turn. Voila, a motorcycle cop parked just a few yards up that street waves for me to pull over. My mind raced as I tried to figure out what I had done wrong. Nothing that I could imagine. I roll down my window and the officer asks me if I had seen the street sign posted at the corner. I indicated that I've seen the signs there many times, including that for example you can't park along that street during the morning and evening commutes. He says to me, not those signs, the new one. Huh? Well, they had just put up a temporary sign that said that for the next two weeks there is no right-turn on red allowed between the hours of 5:30 p.m. to 7:30 p.m. on weekday evenings.

I grumbled to myself as he wrote the ticket, and he simultaneously pulled over a dozen other cars. This was going to be a bonanza for the Los Angeles city coffers. I drove around the block because I wanted to see this temporary sign. It was mounted onto a sign post that already had five other signs on it. Only someone that was directly looking at the post and that was intent on reading all five signs would have realized that the temporary one even existed. Friends thought I should go to court and fight the ticket, but I decided that there was no point in trying to fight city hall on this one.

Why all this rambling about a road sign? Because road signs are going to be crucial to the success of self-driving cars. I realize that such a statement seems odd on the face of things. How could old-fashion road signs make any difference to state-of-the-art self-driving cars. It's simple. Self-driving cars need to obey the traffic laws and so they need to know what the signs say in order to comply with them. For those of you that instantly retort that in this electronic age that it is ridiculous to rely upon road signs, I can only say that until we are able to replace road signs with electronic versions, they are still the ruling kings of the road. The cost to replace conventional road signs with electronics ones is pretty high and so don't hold your breath that we'll suddenly see an overhaul of road signs to become digitally based.

You might also be thinking that certainly all road signs must already be captured someplace electronically, such as via Google's mapping of the roads. You'd be surprised. There are indeed lots and lots of pictures and video that have roads signs somewhere embedded in them, but there is no nationwide and nor global database that has the road signs information electronically available for access. It is still the "I'll know it when I see it" circumstance, namely as you drive down a road you'll see a road sign and have to figure out what it says.

Plus, even if we did a snapshot in time, like let's say we scanned Google road images captured a year ago, think about my example above of when I got nabbed. It was a road sign put up for just two weeks. These kinds of signs are popping up all the time. Now, I am not saying that in the entire realm of road signs that the new ones and the temporary ones are a big chunk, but it is just that even if you had the road signs in pictures and video, you'd still be looking at just one snapshot in time.

Speaking of which, you might be tempted to believe that you could just use a massive neural network to look at the pictures and videos of roads and readily find the road signs. This is not as easy as it sounds. Road signs are notorious for being obscured by tree branches. They are often covered in graffiti. They are bent by kids that like to hang on the signs. They are twisted away from the road and you can only catch a glimpse at it based on your angle of approach. They are sometimes hanging loose and the writing is weather worn. If you've ever seen the standard road signs shown in a book or driving guide, you know from real-world driving that they are rarely so pristine and readable.

Therefore, even if we had images of that street sign down there on Mulberry street, the odds of easily doing an automated scan to determine what it means is problematic. That's the reason why AI can help out. Just as AI and machine learning can review thousands upon thousands of images of cats, and then generalize to what a cat looks like, similarly we can do the same with street signs. A startup called Mapillary is trying to do a crowdsourced approach to collecting photos from around the world of streets, which could potentially be used to have machine learning learn about street signs. They claim to have already collected 116,140,578 photos covering 2,462,653,892 meters of area. They allow a limited amount of free access to the data set and then charge for more access.

Here's ultimately what we might have evolve about street signs and self-driving cars. There will be some enterprising entrepreneurs that put together AI-based systems that learn how to read street signs. Those making the self-driving cars will either tap into that aspect by licensing from those firms, or maybe buy such a firm, or maybe opt to do the same thing themselves. Either way, a self-driving car while driving will need to use its sensors, primarily cameras, in order to detect a road sign by its overall shape and position, and then flow the image over to its internal AI-specialist component that can figure out what the road sign says. Then, the road sign information will be relayed to the overarching self-driving car AI, which will take into account whatever the road sign purports to indicate.

The self-driving car might alter its plan of action based on the contents of the sign. For example, suppose the sign says the speed limit is 35 miles per hour. The self-driving car maybe was coming down a hill where it had just been going 45 miles per hour, and now has to reduce speed to accommodate the 35 mph. In other cases, the road sign might not invoke any reaction by the self-driving car. Where I live, there is a tsunami sign posted on the coast road that I use to get to work. I am guessing that the self-driving car would not need to take into account that the car itself is in a tsunami zone, though if the self-driving car can also turn into a boat then I had better buy one in case I encounter a tsunami.

In the future, the multitude of self-driving cars on the road might end-up solving the street signs recognition problem by sharing with other self-driving cars what they know about the street signs. I am not sure whether this is going to happen per se, since it might be that one maker of a self-driving car might want to claim that their self-driving car is better than other competing self-driving cars because it does a better job of recognizing street signs, and so they presumably would not want to share what their AI system knows about street signs.

You might laugh at the notion that when you go to buy a self-driving car that it might be distinctive by an ability to read street signs, but I wouldn't be so quick to think it silly. Keep in mind that if we actually get to a situation where all cars are self-driving cars, somehow each maker has to find a means to make you want to buy their self-driving car over some other brand. It probably won't be sold on the features we think of for today's cars, and so a high-quality highly reliable street sign detector might just be one key factor that sways you toward the one brand that has it. Can't you see the ads for this, broadcast during the Super Bowl, showcasing an "inferior" self-driving car that zooms past a sign that says "Sinkhole ahead" while the advertiser's self-driving car comes to a halt to avoid the deathtrap. I ask you, which self-driving car would you want to buy?

CHAPTER 19

PARKING YOUR CAR

THE AI WAY

CHAPTER 19

PARKING YOUR CAR
THE AI WAY

When you are using a car to get you from point A to point B, it is a blessing in that you are able to move along rapidly and get to your destination expeditiously. The hitch or curse often occurs once you get to your destination and realize that there is no place to park your car. Besides the obvious frustration of driving around and around to find a place to park, there are adverse environmental consequences in that the amount of fuel consumed and pollution generated are due to simply wanting to park your automobile. Wouldn't it be nice if you could somehow magically be always able to park your car, doing so without the usual dance of darting for an open spot and having to play chicken with other cars vying for the same spot of turf.

There are several ways in which AI is coming to the aid of the car parking problem. Let's take a look at the various ways that AI is being applied, and I hope it will bolster your spirits that soon and someday the parking issue will be resolved. You can dream at night that one day you'll never get a parking ticket again, and that your car getting towed because you parked in that red zone won't have to happen anymore.

AI Parks Your Car

AI is being used to actually park your car. There are a number of car brands that have specific models that can park the car autonomously, including the Lincoln MKS, Mercedes-Benz E-Class, Ford Focus, Toyota Prius, Chrysler 200, Tesla Model S, BMW i3,

Chevrolet Malibu and others. The first such capability began to appear commercially around 2003.

If you've ever watched a car do its own parallel parking, it is a marvel to watch, though also a bit nail biting at times. The car abides by the usual practice of lining up and backing into a tight spot. For drivers that are nervous about doing parallel parking themselves, it is wondrous to see the car fit into a viable spot. But, some tolerances for the AI are set to not allow parallel parking in really tight circumstances, and so a human that wants to brave possibly banging against other cars might need to take over the controls from the AI system to squeeze into a narrow opening.

The use of AI to park a car will continue to be adopted into all cars. Right now, the cost of the hardware and software elements makes it prohibitive for all cars, but we can expect that gradually it will become as ubiquitous as other features such as cruise control has become. One advantage of the AI capability is that it allows for parking in spots that a human might have not thought they could get into, and so in some sense it does increase the utilization of parking spots. That being said, the AI right now is generally not able to determine whether you are parking in a legally allowed spot, and so it is up to the human to figure out whether they are legally doing so. Even if the car parks you into a parallel parking opportunity, if the road has street sweeping that afternoon and your car is parked there, you are going to get a ticket.

AI Identifies Where To Park

The above aspects of having an AI system park your car does not address the issue of trying to find a spot to park. In other words, once you've found a spot, then the AI helps to park the car, but what about knowing where car parking even exists? There's an app for that.

There is a myriad of apps that have appeared for helping with finding a parking space. Some of them are based on the wisdom-of-the-crowd, namely that people using the mobile app are kindly marking electronically via the app where there are parking spots and which ones are open. There is also a monetary angle too, involving some apps that allow one person that is holding a parking space to offer it for bid to other drivers that are wanting that parking space. Some cities have opted to ban or otherwise regulate such apps, doing so because they are worried that only those that are wealthy enough can garner choice parking spots, and also concerned that there might become a profession of parking-spot-holder (a person that makes a living entirely by sitting in high-demand parking spots and then selling them throughout the day to harried drivers).

Even more recently, AI has been added to the army of ways to find a parking spot. At the start of this month of February 2017, a new feature was added into Google Maps for Android, making use of machine learning to predict parking difficulties. Right now, it only encompasses 25 major US cities. Ultimately, Google intends to have the feature on a more widespread basis. Allow me a moment to explain what it does and why it is helping to solve a rather complex problem.

Let's begin with exploring parking spot data. There is very little real-time information about open parking spots. Seldom do you see any Internet-connected parking meters that will report whether they are at a spot that is available or occupied. Of course, these "dumb" parking meters only know whether someone put money into the meter or not, and there are often scofflaws that park in a metered spot and have not paid for the privilege. Thus, even if we had tons of these web-based Internet-of-Things (IoT) meters, there would not be any guarantee that an open spot is really open. Newer "smart" parking meters are being designed to detect whether a car is present and be able to do other wizardry aspects related to car parking and paying for parking.

Google engineers realized that to obtain "ground truth data" (meaning data that reflects the reality of parking spots), they would have to find some other source for it. They were able to entice users to share their parking-related location data, via crowdsourcing, and built-up a parking related database that contains anonymous aggregated data. This can be used in many clever ways. For example, suppose you had entered that you wanted to go to the diner on Mulberry Street, and when you arrived there you were unable to park, so you drove around the block to find a spot. The machine learning that Google applied to the database was able to discern this kind of effort, and therefore reasonably conclude that parking on Mulberry Street at the diner is tough to find.

The machine learning also had to take into account factors such as day of the week and time of the day. Maybe parking on Mulberry Street is impossible at lunch time on a weekday, but wide open in the afternoon and weekends. Currently, the Google Maps feature does not tell you whether or where a parking spot is open. Instead, it tells you the likelihood of finding a parking spot at a particular destination. And, it can also indicate alternative areas nearby that are frequently used by those trying to park at your desired destination. Take a look at the Google Research Blog for the "Using Machine Learning to Predict Parking Difficulty" piece written by James Cook, Yechen Li, and Ravi Kumar for further info about what this new feature does.

Self-Driving Cars To The Rescue

Once we have self-driving cars, there are some that predict that we will no longer have any parking related problems. Their prediction is based on the simple notion that you can have your self-driving car drop you at your destination, and it will then forage for a place to park. This reduces your frustration about parking because your car is taking on the task entirely for you.

I would argue that it is more complicated than that, and such easy answers aren't always right. Let's follow the logic of the parking situation for self-driving cars. Yes, the self-driving car can wander off to find a parking spot. Indeed, some believe that tight city space will no longer need to use up land for parking, since the self-driving car can go wherever else needed to get a parking spot. This has some truth to it, but we need to also consider how far away do you want your self-driving car to go? If the self-driving car drives an hour away to get a parking spot, this is consuming fuel and polluting to do so, plus it also means that when you want to leave you'll need to have it come back another hour's distance.

If you are working in downtown and you know for sure that you'll be in the office for an eight-hour shift, it might make sense to have your car wander far away. Suppose though that you have an emergency or something else unexpected arises, again your car is far away. Generally, it seems doubtful that having your self-driving car park some long ways away is going to make much sense. In that case, there will still need to be parking somewhat nearby to destinations that humans find popular.

Fortunately, we are likely going to be able to use parking spots more efficiently with the advent of self-driving cars. For example, a parking structure that allows for human drivers to park cars needs to accommodate the driving wildness of human drivers, while if it parks only self-driving cars then the parking structure can be more compact and streamlined. Predictions by some futurists is that we'll be able to cram more parked cars into less space and thus free-up some amount of inner city space devoted to parking.

To conclude this topic for now, I'll bring up one other hope about parking. Flying cars. If we had flying cars, they would presumably need to be parked someplace (other than hovering in the air), and so again we have many of the same aspects to consider as the self-driving car. There are differences though between a ground-based self-driving car and a flying self-driving car, in that the flying version can park in places that ground-based cars can't easily reach and they can get to further away distances much more quickly. Don't be surprised if you see that I have started up a new business, Lance's Cloud Parking, wanting to be the first to provide parking in the sky for self-driving flying cars.

Lance B. Eliot

CHAPTER 20

NOT FAST ENOUGH: HUMAN FACTORS IN SELF-DRIVING CARS

CHAPTER 20

NOT FAST ENOUGH: HUMAN FACTORS IN SELF-DRIVING CARS

You are driving your car and suddenly a child darts into the street from the sidewalk. You see the child in the corner of your eye, your mental processes calculate that the car could hit the child, and you then realize you should make an evasive move. Your mind races as you try to decide whether you should slam on the brakes, or swerve away, or both, or maybe instead try to speed-up and get past the child before your car intersects with him. As your mind weighs each option, your hands seemingly grab the steering wheel with a death-like grip and your foot hoovers above the accelerator and brake pedal, awaiting a command from your mind. Finally, after what seems like an eternity, you push mightily on the brakes and come to halt within inches of the child. Everyone is Okay, but it was scary for driver and child.

How long did the above scenario take to play out? Though it took several sentences to describe and thus might seem like it took forever, the reality is that the whole situation took just a few seconds of time. Terrifying time. Crucial time. If you had been distracted, perhaps holding your cellphone in your hand and trying to text a message to order a pizza for dinner, you would have had even less time to react. Driving a car involves lots of relatively boring time, such as cruising on the freeway when there is no other traffic, but it also involves moments of sheer terror and second-by-second split-second decision making and hand-foot coordination.

This ability to react to a driving situation is an essential element of AI-based self-driving cars, specifically self-driving cars that are relying on human drivers to help out (there are some self-driving cars that intend to remove human drivers entirely out-of-the-loop, but most are not, at least right now). For self-driving cars that expect the human driver to be ready to take over the controls, the developers of such self-driving cars had better be thinking clearly about the Human Computer Interaction (HCI) factors involved in the boundary between human drivers and AI-automation driving the car.

Suppose that an AI-automation was driving the car in the above child-darts-into-street scenario. Perhaps the AI-automation is "smart" enough to make a decision and avoid hitting the child. But, suppose the AI-automation determines that it is unable to find a solution that avoids hitting the child, and so it then opts to hand over the controls to the human driver. Depending upon how much time the AI-automation has already consumed, the time leftover for the human driver to comprehend the situation and then react might be below, maybe even far below, the amount of time needed for the human mental calculations and hand-foot processes to be performed.

A recent study by Alexander Eriksson and Neville Stanton at the University of Southampton tries to shed light on what kinds of reaction times we're talking about (their study was published in the *Human Factors: The Journal of the Human Factors and Ergonomics Society* on January 26, 2017). They undertook a study using a car simulator, and had 26 participants (10 female, 16 male; ranging in ages from 20 to 52, with an average record of 10.57 years of normal driving experience) try to serve as a human driver for a self-driving car. In this capacity, the experiment's subjects sat awaiting the self-driving car to hand over control to them, and they then had to react accordingly. The simulation pretended that the car was going 70 miles per hour, meaning that for every second of reaction time that the car would move ahead by about 102 feet.

They setup the scenario with two situations, one wherein the human driver was focused on the self-driving car and the roadway, and in the second situation they asked the human driver to read passages from the *National Geographic* (now that's rather dry reading!). In the case of the non-distracted situation, the humans had a median reaction time of 4.56 seconds, while in the distracted situation it was 6.06 seconds.

Though it is expected that the reaction time for the distracted situation would be longer, it is also somewhat misleading to focus solely on the reaction times. I say this because the reaction time was how long it took for them to take back control of the car. Meanwhile, the time it took for them to take some kind of action ranged from 1.9 seconds to 25.7 seconds.

Let me repeat that last important point. Taking back control of a self-driving car might be relatively quick, but taking the right action might take a lot longer. Regardless though about the right action, notice that it took about 5-6 seconds to even take over manual control of the car. That's precious seconds that could spell life-or-death (and a distance of roughly 500-600 feet at the 70 mph speed), since either a collision or incident might happen in that time frame (or distance), or it might mean that the time now leftover prior to a collision or incident is beyond your ability to avert the danger.

We should also keep in mind that this was only in a simulated car. The participants were likely much more attentive than they would be in a real car. They knew they were there for a driving test of some kind, and so they were also on-alert in a manner that the everyday driver is likely not. All in all, the odds are that any similar study of driving on real roads would discover a much longer reaction time, I'd be willing to bet.

Let's consider some of the salient aspects of the Human Factors Interaction involved with a self-driving car and a human driver:

No Viable Solution

If the AI-based system of the self-driving car cannot arrive at a solution to the driving problem, it could mean that there just isn't any viable solution at all. Thus, handing the car driving over to the human is like saying, here, have at it, good luck pal. This is a no-win circumstance. The human driver is not really being given an option and instead simply being passed the buck.

Hidden Problem

The AI-based system might "know" that a child is darting from the sidewalk, but when it hands control over to the human the question arises as to how the human will know this. Yes, the human driver is supposed to be paying attention, but it could be that the human driver cannot see the child at all (suppose the AI-based system used a radar capability, but that visually the child is unseen by the human). In essence, these self-driving cars are not giving any hints or clues to the human driver about what has caused the urgency, and it is up to the human driver to be omniscient and figure it out.

Cognition Dissonance

This is similar to the Hidden Problem, in that the context of the problem is not known by the human, but suppose the human makes an assumption that the reason the self-driving car is handing over the control is because there is a trash truck up ahead that needs to be avoided, and meanwhile it is actually because the car is about to hit the child. There is a gap, or dissonance, between what the human is aware of and what the AI-based system is aware of.

Reaction Time

We've covered this one already, namely, the amount of time needed for the human to regain control of the car, plus the amount of time needed for the human to then take proper action. The AI-based system has to hand-over control with some semblance of realizing how much time a human might take to figure out what is going on and also have time to still be able to take needed action.

Controls Access

A human driver might have put their feet aside of the brake and accelerator, or might have their hands reaching behind the passenger seat to grab a candy bar. Thus, even if they are mentally aware that the self-driving car is telling them to take the controls, their physical appendages are not able to readily do so. This is a controls access issue and one that should be considered for the design of self-driving cars in terms of the steering wheel and the pedals.

False Reaction

This is one aspect that not many researchers have considered and certainly none or seemingly none of the self-driving car makers seem to have been contemplating. Here's the case. You are a human driver, you get comfortable with a self-driving car, but you also know that at some random moment, often when you least expect it, the AI-based system is going to shove the controls back to you. As such, for some drivers, they will potentially be on the edge of their seat and anxious for that moment to arise. This could also then cause eager-beaver drivers to take back control when the AI-based system has not alerted them, and the human might make a sudden maneuver because they think the car is headed towards danger. The human is falsely reacting to an unannounced and non-issue. The human could dangerously swerve off the road or flip the car, doing so because they thought it was time to take sudden action.

CONCLUSION

Overall, the rush toward self-driving cars is more so focused on getting the self-driving car to drive, rather than also focusing on the balance between the human driver and the AI-based system. There needs to be a carefully thought through and choreographed interplay between the two. When a takeover request is lobbed to the human (these are called TOR's in self-driving parlance), there needs to be a proper allocation of TORLT (TOR Lead Time). Without getting the whole human-computer equation appropriately developed, we're going to have self-driving cars that slam into people and the accusatory finger will be pointed at a human driver, which, might be unfair in that the human might have actually been attentive and willing to help, but for whom the self-driving car provided no reasonable way to immerse the human in helping out. We can't let the robots toss a live hand grenade to a human. Humans and their alignment with the AI-based computer factors will be vital for our joint success. Think about this the next time you are the human driver in a self-driving car.

CHAPTER 21

STATE OF GOVERNMENT

REPORTING ON

SELF-DRIVING CARS

CHAPTER 21

STATE OF GOVERNMENT ON
SELF-DRIVING CARS

The new phonebook is here! The new phonebook is here!

You might recall that comedian Steve Martin made that famous exclamation in his now-classic movie *The Jerk*. He was referring to seeing his name in-print (well, his movie character's name), and being excited to know that he had finally made it to the big time. Likewise, last week the California Department of Motor Vehicles (DMV) released its eagerly awaited collection of so-called "disengagement" reports that were filed by companies that had registered to test their self-driving cars in California. The collection covered the time period of December 2015 to November 2016, and eleven companies filed reports: BMW, Bosch, GM's Cruise Automation, Delphi Automotive Systems, Ford, Google – Waymo, Honda, Nissan North America, Mercedes-Benz, Tesla Motors, and Volkswagon Group of America.

So, I'll say it, the new disengagement reports are here! The new disengagement reports are here! The reason these are worthy of rapt attention is that they help reveal the latest status of self-driving cars. The numbers provided are self-reported by the companies, and presumably forthright (else they'd be violating the DMV regulations), though there isn't any independent third-party verification per se of their reported claims. I am not suggesting that any of the reports are false. Actually, the bigger issue is that the DMV opted to allow for flexibility in reporting, and so it is not readily feasible to compare the numbers reported by the companies. It's a shame that a regulator (the California DMV) on the one hand has insisted on annual reporting, which I argue is handy, but at the same time the regulator did not provide clear-cut standards for doing the reporting. It is like a football game involving teams that pretty much get to make up the rules and therefore you cannot compare them on the basis of touchdowns, since some of teams are using 6 points for a touchdown while others are using say 4 points for a touchdown.

The California DMV needs to tighten up the reporting requirements. That being said, California's DMV should be applauded for even requiring such reporting, while other states such as Michigan, Florida, Arizona, and Nevada are not. I don't want to seemingly besmirch California for failing to offer clearer reporting requirements and somehow lose sight of the fact that most of the other states don't require any reporting at all. To me, those states deserve an even harsher lashing. California has done the right thing, forcing the companies that want to test their self-driving cars on the public roadways to come forth with how well it is coming along and how much of such testing they are doing. I realize that some might argue that this is an over-intrusive requirement on these companies, and some might say that it discourages those companies from testing. Given that some states aren't requiring the reporting, companies that want to keep secret their testing are sliding over to those states and avoiding having to publish their status. Or, in California, they stay off the public roads and do their testing only on private lands (a somewhat clever or some say sneaky way around the rules). I won't focus further on the public policy implications here, and just note that it is a factor to keep in mind about how self-driving cars are evolving and what the states are doing about it.

What do the numbers show? Google's Waymo reported that their self-driving cars logged about 636,000 miles in California on public roadways during the reporting time period. That's a staggeringly high number in comparison to the other ten companies, which combined together were a mere fraction of that number of miles. For total miles logged and reported, Waymo was about 97% of the miles and the other ten were about 3%. GM's Cruise Automation came in at the #2 spot in terms of most number of miles, indicating about 9,850 miles during the reporting time period. Some companies, such as Honda and Volkswagon, reported zero miles and indicated that they had not done testing on California's public roadways during the reporting time period (at least as far as they interpret what the DMV regulation encompasses).

This brings us to one of the reporting metrics problems. The number of miles driven is a quite imperfect measure since it is important to point out that a mile of open highway is not the same driving complexity as a mile of inner city street-clogged bumper-busting traffic. Not all miles were created equal, some aptly say. If I have my self-driving car use open highways where there is little human-like navigation required, this is a far cry from the human-like capability needed in more onerous traffic conditions. For example, much of Waymo's mileage is apparently in the Mountain View area, along suburban streets. I would contend that these kinds of miles are a lot "easier" than say downtown San Francisco driving.

I'll also point out something else that I've observed while in the Mountain View area. I've seen the Waymo cars quite often. I have also noticed that other human-driven cars are tending to give a lot of latitude to the Waymo cars nowadays (which are standouts due to their now well-known iconic shape and sensory gear). I mention this aspect because the next metric I am going to discuss is the disengagements counts. Waymo reported that they had a relatively tiny number of disengagements, indicating they had 124 in total, which seems pretty darned good when you also consider that their self-driving cars went 636,000 miles or so. It is a good sign, but at the same time, I wonder how much of this is due to the fact that human drivers are changing their behavior to allow the self-driving car to drive without having to deal with true traffic conditions (i.e., humans not driving as wildly as they normally do). And, these cars are driving repeatedly on the same roads, over and over. This is vastly different from having to navigate more unfamiliar territory and figure out the idiosyncrasies of roads you've not been on before.

What does the word "disengagement" actually mean, you might be wondering? According to the California DMV, a disengagement involves the test driver taking over immediate manual control of the vehicle during a testing activity on a public road in California, and doing so because the test driver believed the vehicle had a technological failure or because they thought the self-driving car was not operating in a safe manner. This might seem like an airtight definition. It is actually full of tons of loopholes. Let's start with taking over immediate manual control. For some companies, their viewpoint is that if the test driver waits say more than a few seconds then this is not considered an "immediate" circumstance and so is not counted as a disengagement. Is this a fair or unfair interpretation? Again, it should not be open to interpretation and a clearer standard should exist.

I can also imagine that there might be pressure placed on the human test drivers to avoid doing a disengagement. In essence, if you are a self-driving car company and you know that ultimately the whole world will be examining your number of disengagements, you would probably want to seek the minimal number that you can. This is not to suggest that anyone is telling test drivers to allow themselves to be put in jeopardy or jeopardize others on the road. It is simply another element to consider that the test drivers will each vary as to why and when they think a disengagement is warranted. Thus, again, the disengagement metric is not a reliably standardized metric. Tesla reported 550 miles in total, and 182 disengagements, which suggests that they had about 1 disengagement every 3 miles driven. This would seem at first glance like a scary number. But, you need to keep in mind the number of miles, the conditions involved, how the disengagements were counted, etc.

I have been especially irked by some of the national and worldwide reporting about the California DMV disengagement reports. One bold headline was that numbers don't lie and that the reports presumably prove that self-driving cars are nearly ready to hit the roads unattended. This claim that numbers don't lie is a sadly simplistic suggestion, and I think that all readers should recall the famous line of British Prime Minister Benjamin Disraeli: "There are three kinds of lies: lies, damned lies, and statistics." Another irksome headline was that the disengagement reports show that there are 2,500 or so problems with self-driving cars. This is a total of the number of disengagements reported, but it is disingenuous to suggest that somehow the count implies that self-driving cars had 2,500 "problems" per se. Yes, a disengagement might have occurred because a self-driving car had a system failure, but it also could be that the test driver felt uncomfortable entrusting the self-driving car in a dicey traffic condition and so decided to take over manual control.

Please be cautious in interpreting the disengagement reporting. I will end on a more macroscopic note about self-driving cars, namely that we need to establish the equivalent of a Turing Test for self-driving cars. In AI, we all know that the Turing Test is a handy means to try and ascertain whether a system appears to embody human intelligence, doing so by trying to see whether humans can distinguish whether or not a system is interacting in a human intelligence-like fashion. Though imperfect as a test, it nonetheless is a means to assess AI-based systems.

A Level 5 self-driving car, which is considered the topmost of self-driving cars and implies that a self-driving car can be driven by automation in whatever same manner that a human can, there isn't any specific testing protocol for this. Do we just let a self-driving car drive for a thousand miles and if it does not need any disengagements, do we safely conclude it is a true Level 5? Or do we let it drive for 100,000 miles? As I've mentioned herein, miles alone is not sufficient, and disengagement is imperfect too. We need a more comprehensive, standardized test that could be applied to self-driving cars. If someone else doesn't do it, I will, and I'll probably call it the Eliot Test. You could be immortalized if you come up with one instead.

CHAPTER 22

THE HEAD NOD PROBLEM FOR SELF-DRIVING CARS

CHAPTER 22

THE HEAD NOD PROBLEM
FOR SELF-DRIVING CARS

I drove up to a four-way stop in my neighborhood the other day, and arrived just as another car happened to arrive (catty-corner of me). There we were, two cars and their human drivers, trying to ascertain which of us would proceed next. You've undoubtedly been in this same kind of stand-off. Should you go ahead, or should you wait for the other driver to proceed? You might inch forward, hoping to suggest you want to go first. Meanwhile, the other car inches forward too. Realizing that you both were starting to roll forward, you both abruptly come to a complete stop again. How long will this last? We might stay this way for a minute, five minutes, or maybe five years.

Finally, by a head nod, I signaled subtly to the other driver that he could make passage safely through the intersection and I would wait accordingly. The other driver hit the gas and went along his merry way. Accident averted. Another world crisis solved. By the rules-of-the-road in my state, he admittedly had right-of-way since the rule is that if two cars arrive at the four-way at the same moment in time, the one to the right gets to proceed. I think we were both unsure of whether we had exactly both arrived at the same instant of time. Neither of us wanted to make a leap in judgement that could produce a collision. I was not in a hurry and so was willing to just wait as long as needed to have the other driver go ahead.

This brings us to the topic of self-driving cars. You might be aware that some of the early trials of self-driving cars on-the-road were somewhat comical due to the four-way stop kind of circumstance. A self-driving car came up to a similar stop, and waited for the other car to proceed. In some cases, the other car, being driven by a human, opted to wait and see what the self-driving car would do (rightfully so, since one should be justifiably suspicious of these experimental self-driving cars). Thus, both cars just sat there for an inordinate amount of time, each waiting for the other to proceed.

There were also cases of a self-driving car coming up to a stop and then detected that the other car was going ahead by essentially refusing to stop completely, so the self-driving car waited, even if it had right-of-way by the rules. Of course, as happens often at peak traffic periods, another human driven car came up to the four-way intersection, stopped just ever so briefly (a so-called "rolling stop" in cop parlance), and once again the self-driving car continued to remain stationary. Car after car, driven by humans, proceeded to do the same, and the self-driving car sat motionless since it refused to try and play chicken with these human driven cars.

Though perhaps comical, it brings up an important factor about self-driving cars and AI. Those early developers of those self-driving cars complained that humans are "bad" drivers and that it is the fault of those humans that the self-driving car got in a pickle. They further lamented that those darned humans should get off-the-road, and once we all have self-driving cars, and there are no human driven cars, there won't be any need to worry about this issue. The self-driving cars will presumably stick to the letter of the law and so there won't be any ambiguity about what is supposed to happen. To these remarks, I have but one word: dreamers!

There are an estimated 250 million cars in the United States alone, and I can assure you they are not going to magically be set aside for self-driving cars overnight. It will be years and years before those cars are replaced with self-driving cars and/or augmented to become self-driving cars (which is unlikely for various technical reasons).

In essence, any self-respecting self-driving car is going to have to learn how to deal with human driven cars. That's a fact. If self-driving cars aren't able to contend with human driven cars, you might as well then put your forecast for self-driving cars to become so far in the future that we can't even see that date from here. There is going to be a mixture on-the-road of self-driven cars and human driven cars, at least for the foreseeable future (maybe someday this won't be the case, but realistically it will be an instrumental and inevitable interim step toward a possible all-and-only self-driving car future). Sure, some cities are going to perhaps consider having some roads designated for human drivers and other roads for self-driving cars, in an effort to separate the two, but this "solution" is not especially tenable and exceedingly costly, so as to be impracticable generally.

It is a core principle that self-driving cars will need to be able to predict and deal with human driving idiosyncrasies. Furthermore, a robust self-driving car should also be able to deal *directly* with humans. By dealing directly, I am referring to the head nod. In my story above about coming to the four-way stop, the other driver looked at me, I looked at the other driver. We made eye contact, from afar. He saw me nod my head. He interpreted this to mean I was relinquishing the roadway to him. Humans do this all the time. It can literally be a head nod, or it could be a waving of the hand, or a mouthing of words, or even just a staring look of the eyes (you know, that piercing look that says go ahead even if I think you are a jerk, laden with emotion). Some of the software and hardware developers for self-driving cars are entirely missing the mark about this aspect, and they are not taking into account the human driver-to-driver communication that happens continually while driving our cars.

How can this head nod problem be dealt with? Sensors on the self-driving cars include sonar, radar, and other capabilities, including for some there are cameras on-board too. Via sensor data fusion, the AI of self-driving car tries to examine what is going on and make decisions about how to drive the car. The cameras are usually looking for things like a cow standing in the road, or a child's ball that rolled into the street. These cameras also need to be able to visually detect other drivers, which is a vital element that needs to be included in any truly realistic self-driving cars. I know that some self-driving car developers will wince at this notion, since they are already so busy with trying to program so many other self-driving car technical matters. Plus, as mentioned earlier, some of those developers are still using the simplistic belief that self-driving cars will take over the roads and therefore there aren't going to be human drivers to deal with anyway.

I assert that the head nod problem is real, it is going to exist, it must be dealt with, and self-driving car developers should be coping with it. We already know that some of the underlying capabilities exist, for example consider how Facebook has popularly been able to do facial recognition to find your friends hidden in your Bahamas pictures that you posted. Indeed, there is a hot trend now of doing sentiment analysis of faces. You walk into a store to look at the latest shirts, and a camera captures your facial image, does a sentiment analysis, and maybe the retailer discovers that most people make an ugly face when they look at the shirts (probably time to redesign those Hawaiian prints). We can build upon this kind of facial and human expression recognition, and begin to tackle the head nod problem head-on. It is an undeniably thorny problem because it involves the subtleties of human movement and interaction, the moving of the head or arms, the waving of hands, etc. I am confident it can be figured out.

That being said, one question I often get asked involves how does the self-driving car respond? Unless we have android human-looking robots driving the car, there is no place for the human driver to vent their frustrations and not a ready means for the self-driving car to wave back or do a similar head nod. Imagine for a moment if we were having human-looking robots that drove self-driving cars, then it would be a human-to-robot style of communication. Logically, it might lead to some incredible road rage that might ensue — you can just imagine a human driver and a robot driver, they get out of their cars to settle a roadway dispute, and go to fists at the side of the road, angry over who did what while driving their cars. Fortunately, we aren't heading in that direction with our self-driving cars.

The reality for self-driving cars is that humans will be willing to make faces and gestures in the direction of the self-driving, regardless whether there are robotic eyes and hands waving back at them. A camera can detect these human responses by human drivers. Too, the self-driving cars will likely be outfitted with some exterior signaling to communicate toward the human driver. Keep in mind that all of this head nodding and discussion about the role of human drivers and self-driving cars is still nascent, and for many of the self-driving cars manufacturers and developers it is barely on their radar. They are trying to get the basics going first. I predict that those that are the more forward thinking are or will soon be working on the head nod problem. Nod your head if you agree.

CHAPTER 23

CES REVEALS

SELF-DRIVING CARS

DIFFERENCES

CHAPTER 23

CES REVEALS SELF-DRIVING CAR DIFFERENCES

At the Consumer Electronics Show (CES) of January 5–8, 2017, the Self-Driving Technology Marketplace in the Las Vegas Convention Center (LVCC) had increased by 42% over 2016, expanding to encompass the now myriad of car companies, tech companies, and ride-sharing companies that are all seeking the holy grail of producing a self-driving car. Major automakers including BMW, Mercedes Benz, Nissan, Ford, Chrysler, Hyundai, Honda, Toyota and others were there in great force, offering the latest glimpse at where they believe self-driving cars are heading.

Besides showcasing futuristic cars at their oversized and crowd luring booths, some of the companies even provided a "ride and drive" experience outside the LVCC (a sometimes-alarming road drive by a self-driven car on the streets of Las Vegas). Though the opportunity to be a passenger in a self-driving car was an exciting prospect for the attendees (there were often lengthy lines and waits to try one), there were also many reported indications of self-driving cars that had to be taken over by their "emergency" human driver to avoid mishaps and roadway accidents.

Despite the loud hype that self-driving cars are nearly ready for prime time, the reality is that we are still years away from seeing true self-driving cars. A true self-driving car is often defined as being a Level 5 on the scale of self-driving cars established by the Society for Automotive Engineers (SAE) and as sanctioned by the federal government, and consists of a car that can be driven entirely without any human intervention. In short, anything a human driver can do, a self-driving car that is rated as a Level 5 must be able to do. Currently, most of the self-driving cars under development are rated at a level 3 or 4 which allows for some amount of human intervention in the car driving activity.

One key design difference between the many self-driving car initiatives is the fundamental aspect of what the AI/Human role should be. For Google's Waymo self-driving car, they are aiming at an all-AI and no-human role in the driving of the car. This means that there are no controls within the car for the human occupant. There isn't a steering wheel, there isn't a brake pedal, there isn't an accelerator pedal. The human is along for the ride and has no part in the driving of the car.

Nissan is also aiming ultimately at no internal controls for human occupants, but takes a different slant at the role of humans in driving of the self-driving car. In particular, Nissan envisions a remote-control capability of self-driving cars involving humans in some far-flung operations center that can take over your self-driving car when the AI cannot figure out what to do. Borrowing from the NASA Mars rover capabilities, Nissan showed that it is adopting a NASA-created system that will allow remotely situated human operators to be invoked when the self-driven car gets stymied.

Called the Seamless Autonomous Mobility (SAM) system, it is Nissan's answer for the aspect that we don't yet really know whether or when AI will be strong enough to always autonomously drive a car. Nissan even has a catchy slogan for their futuristic cars, namely a goal of zero emissions (being all-electric vehicles) and zero fatalities (due to the self-driving and remote operations capabilities).

Ford showcased a self-driving design that allows for an occupant of the car to still be able to take over the controls of the car. Presumably, the human would do so when alerted by the AI system, or might also do so if for whatever reason the human decided they either had to take the wheel or at least wanted to take over the driving. Hyundai is likewise providing for in-car human operation, plus they are adding a special new function to their cars. The newest trend is a driver mood detection system that tries to discern the emotional state of the driver. By the use of biometric sensors, the AI of the car will adjust the human driver's seat to a different posture, and alter the interior temperature, sounds, lighting, and even generate a scent through the car vents to try and pick-up the mood of the driver.

The mood adjustment features will likely begin to appear on many other car brands as a relatively easy gimmick that can be implemented readily, doing so without having to ensure that a car is an actual self-driving car. Will human drivers want to have their car detect their personal mood and then react by altering the internal environment of the vehicle? Only time will tell whether car buyers and car drivers perceive this mood bending capability as being worthwhile. As I drove back from Vegas, and after having lost quite a bit at the blackjack tables, I am not sure whether even if my car was equipped with a mood adjuster that it would have made me happy. Meanwhile, in terms of what happens in Vegas stays in Vegas, the CES conference showed that what happens in self-driving cars will actually be spreading outside Vegas as we begin to see the latest in AI-based cars hit the roads.

APPENDIX

APPENDIX A
TEACHING WITH THIS MATERIAL

The material in this book can be readily used either as a supplemental to other content for a class, or it can also be used as a core set of textbook material for a specialized class. Classes where this material is most likely used include any classes at the college or university level that want to augment the class by offering thought provoking and educational essays about AI and self-driving cars.

In particular, here are some aspects for class use:

o   Computer Science. Studying AI, autonomous vehicles, etc.

o   Business. Exploring technology and it adoption for business.

o   Sociology. Sociological views on the adoption and advancement of technology.

Specialized classes at the undergraduate and graduate level can also make use of this material.

For each chapter, consider whether you think the chapter provides material relevant to your course topic. There is plenty of opportunity to get the students thinking about the topic and force them to decide whether they agree or disagree with the points offered and positions taken. I would also encourage you to have the students do additional research beyond the chapter material presented (I provide next some suggested assignments they can do).

RESEARCH ASSIGNMENTS ON THESE TOPICS

Your students can find background material on these topics, doing so in various business and technical publications. I list below the top ranked AI related journals. For business publications, I would suggest the usual culprits such as the Harvard Business Review, Forbes, Fortune, WSJ, and the like.

Here are some suggestions of homework or projects that you could assign to students:

a) Assignment for foundational AI research topic: Research and prepare a paper and a presentation on a specific aspect of Deep AI, Machine Learning, ANN, etc. The paper should cite at least 3 reputable sources. Compare and contrast to what has been stated in this book.

b) Assignment for the Self-Driving Car topic: Research and prepare a paper and Self-Driving Cars. Cite at least 3 reputable sources and analyze the characterizations. Compare and contrast to what has been stated in this book.

c) Assignment for a Business topic: Research and prepare a paper and a presentation on businesses and advanced technology. What is hot, and what is not? Cite at least 3 reputable sources. Compare and contrast to the depictions in this book.

d) Assignment to do a Startup: Have the students prepare a paper about how they might startup a business in this realm. They must submit a sound Business Plan for the startup. They could also be asked to present their Business Plan and so should also have a presentation deck to coincide with it.

You can certainly adjust the aforementioned assignments to fit to your particular needs and the class structure. You'll notice that I ask for 3 reputable cited sources for the paper writing based assignments. I usually steer students toward "reputable" publications, since otherwise they will cite some oddball source that has no credentials other than that they happened to write something and post it onto the Internet. You can define "reputable" in whatever way you prefer, for example some faculty think Wikipedia is not reputable while others believe it is reputable and allow students to cite it.

The reason that I usually ask for at least 3 citations is that if the student only does one or two citations they usually settle on whatever they happened to find the fastest. By requiring three citations, it usually seems to force them to look around, explore, and end-up probably finding five or more, and then whittling it down to 3 that they will actually use.

I have not specified the length of their papers, and leave that to you to tell the students what you prefer. For each of those assignments, you could end-up with a short one to two pager, or you could do a dissertation length paper. Base the length on whatever best fits for your class, and the credit amount of the assignment within the context of the other grading metrics you'll be using for the class.

I mention in the assignments that they are to do a paper and prepare a presentation. I usually try to get students to present their work. This is a good practice for what they will do in the business world. Most of the time, they will be required to prepare an analysis and present it. If you don't have the class time or inclination to have the students present, then you can of course cut out the aspect of them putting together a presentation.

If you want to point students toward highly ranked journals in AI, here's a list of the top journals as reported by *various citation counts sources* (this list changes year to year):

- o Communications of the ACM
- o Artificial Intelligence
- o Cognitive Science
- o IEEE Transactions on Pattern Analysis and Machine Intelligence
- o Foundations and Trends in Machine Learning
- o Journal of Memory and Language
- o Cognitive Psychology
- o Neural Networks
- o IEEE Transactions on Neural Networks and Learning Systems
- o IEEE Intelligent Systems
- o Knowledge-based Systems

GUIDE TO USING THE CHAPTERS

For each of the chapters, I provide next some various ways to use the chapter material. You can assign the tasks as individual homework assignments, or the tasks can be used with team projects for the class. You can easily layout a series of assignments, such as indicating that the students are to do item "a" below for say Chapter 1, then "b" for the next chapter of the book, and so on.

a) What is the main point of the chapter and describe in your own words the significance of the topic,

b) Identify at least two aspects in the chapter that you agree with, and support your concurrence by providing at least one other outside researched item as support; make sure to explain your basis for disagreeing with the aspects,

c) Identify at least two aspects in the chapter that you disagree with, and support your disagreement by providing at least one other outside researched item as support; make sure to explain your basis for disagreeing with the aspects,

d) Find an aspect that was not covered in the chapter, doing so by conducting outside research, and then explain how that aspect ties into the chapter and what significance it brings to the topic,

e) Interview a specialist in industry about the topic of the chapter, collect from them their thoughts and opinions, and readdress the chapter by citing your source and how they compared and contrasted to the material,

f) Interview a relevant academic professor or researcher in a college or university about the topic of the chapter, collect from them their thoughts and opinions, and readdress the chapter by citing your source and how they compared and contrasted to the material,

g) Try to update a chapter by finding out the latest on the topic, and ascertain whether the issue or topic has now been solved or whether it is still being addressed, explain what you come up with.

The above are all ways in which you can get the students of your class involved in considering the material of a given chapter. You could mix things up by having one of those above assignments per each week, covering the chapters over the course of the semester or quarter.

As a reminder, here are the chapters of the book and you can select whichever chapters you find most valued for your particular class:

ABOUT THE AUTHOR

Dr. Lance B. Eliot, MBA, PhD is the CEO of Techbruim, Inc., and has over twenty years of industry experience including serving as a corporate officer in a billion dollar firm and was a Partner in a major executive services firm. He is also a serial entrepreneur having founded, ran, and sold several high-tech related businesses. He previously hosted the popular radio show *Technotrends* that was also available on American Airlines flights via their in-flight audio program. Author or co-author of six books and over 300 articles, he has made appearances on CNN, and has been a frequent speaker at industry conferences.

A former professor at the University of Southern California (USC), he founded and led an innovative research lab on Artificial Intelligence in Business. Known as the "AI Insider" his writings on AI advances and trends has been widely read and cited. He also previously served on the faculty of the University of California Los Angeles (UCLA), and was a visiting professor at other major universities. He was elected to the International Board of the Society for Information Management (SIM), a prestigious association of over 3,000 high-tech executives worldwide.

He has performed extensive community service, including serving as Senior Science Adviser to the Vice Chair of the Congressional Committee on Science & Technology. He has served on the Board of the OC Science & Engineering Fair (OCSEF), where he is also has been a Grand Sweepstakes judge, and likewise served as a judge for the Intel International SEF (ISEF). He served as the Vice Chair of the Association for Computing Machinery (ACM) Chapter, a prestigious association of computer scientists. Dr. Eliot has been a shark tank judge for the USC Mark Stevens Center for Innovation on start-up pitch competitions, and served as a mentor for several incubators and accelerators in Silicon Valley and Silicon Beach. He serves on several Boards and Committees at USC, including having served on the Marshall Alumni Association (MAA) Board in Southern California.

Dr. Eliot holds a PhD from USC, MBA, and Bachelor's in Computer Science, and earned the CDP, CCP, CSP, CDE, and CISA certifications. Born and raised in Southern California, and having traveled and lived internationally, he enjoys scuba diving, surfing, and sailing.

ADDENDUM

Advances in AI and Autonomous Vehicles: Cybernetic Self-Driving Cars

Practical Advances in Artificial Intelligence (AI) and Machine Learning

By
Dr. Lance B. Eliot, MBA, PhD

———

For supplemental materials of this book, visit:

www.lance-blog.com

For special orders of this book, contact:

LBE Press Publishing

Email: LBE.Press.Publishing@gmail.com

www.ingramcontent.com/pod-product-compliance
Lightning Source LLC
Chambersburg PA
CBHW051230050326
40689CB00007B/858